The Wideness of God's Mercy

VOLUME TWO

THE WIDENESS OF GOD'S MERCY

Litanies
to Enlarge Our Prayer

Volume Two

Prayers for the World

**An Ecumenical Collection
Compiled and Adapted by**

JEFFERY W. ROWTHORN

The Seabury Press

Library of Congress Catalog Card Number: 84-52316

ISBN: 0-86683-789-2 (two-volume set)
ISBN: 0-86683-794-9 (Volume One)
ISBN: 0-86683-795-7 (Volume Two)

Printed in the United States of America

5 4 3 2 1

Winston Press, Inc.
430 Oak Grove
Minneapolis, Minnesota

For my parents

Eric and Eileen Rowthorn

who by personal example
first taught me
that we are to praise God
not only with our lips
but in our lives.

Contents

PRAYER AND MISSION

The Church

The Christian

The Whole Armor of God

PRAYER AND DAILY LIFE

PRAYER AND SOCIETY

The Nation

War and Peace

Acknowledgments

For permission to reprint material in these volumes, grateful acknowledgment is made to the individuals and publishers named on the pages below:

Abingdon Press for selections from *Lift Up Your Hearts* by Walter Russell Bowie. Copyright renewal © 1976 by Walter Russell Bowie. Used by permission of the publishers, Abingdon Press.

George Allen and Unwin for "The Southwell Litany" by Bishop G. Ridding of Southwell.

Horace T. Allen, Jr. for his "Litany of Dedication."

Allyn and Bacon, Inc., for selections from *The Student Prayer Book* by J. Oliver Nelson, copyright © 1953 by Haddam House, Inc. Edited and written by a Haddam House Committee under the chairmanship of John Oliver Nelson, Association Press, New York, 1953.

American Bible Society for Scripture quotations designated GNB from the *Good News Bible*, the Bible in Today's English Version. Copyright © 1976 by the American Bible Society.

Andrews, McMeel & Parker Inc. for an excerpt from *Prayers from the Burned-Out City* by Robert W. Castle, Jr. Copyright 1968 by Sheed & Ward, Inc. Reprinted with permission of Andrews, McMeel & Parker Inc. All rights reserved.

Ascension Lutheran Church, Baltimore, Maryland, and the Lutheran Church in America, for a litany from *Monday's Ministries: The Ministry of the Laity* by Melvin Vos; edited by Raymond Tiemeyer, Parish Life Press, Philadelphia, 1979.

Augsburg Publishing House for selections reprinted from *Lutheran Book of Worship*, copyright © 1978, by permission of Augsburg Publishing House; for material reprinted by

Introduction

The opening pages of the first volume in this ecumenical collection described the emergence of the litany as the principal vehicle for the Church's intercessory prayer. Slowly, but inexorably, the "Prayers of the People" fell into disuse, however, and the Reformation did little to rectify this neglect of an earlier and universal liturgical practice. This meant that neither in Roman Catholic nor in Protestant congregations were the lay members of the Church able to exercise the priestly ministry which was theirs by virtue of their baptism.

Only recently has this situation changed. Now "the common prayer" or "the prayer of the faithful" is being restored to the regular pattern of Sunday worship in many denominations, and it is hardly surprising that, to achieve this end, the litany is being once more employed as the primary vehicle for the "Prayers of the People."

The introduction to this second volume does not attempt to cover that same ground again. Instead, it seeks to distinguish between the scope and contents of the two books; to demonstrate ways of using the litanies contained in the pages which follow; and to indicate why changes have been made in the text of many of them. It is hoped that this will make this second volume eminently usable without necessary recourse to the first volume.

The litanies in Voume One address themes concerned specifically with the worship and internal life of the Church. Ancient forms of prayer, prayers for the seasons of the Church year, acts of adoration, confession and thanksgiving, and intercession in litany form for the unity and ministry of the Church are all to be found there.

Now, in Volume Two, attention shifts to what might be called the external life of the Church, its mission and witness in the world at large. To demonstrate the Church's calling to care for the life of the world in all its aspects, the litanies which follow are indeed broad in scope. They address such matters as:

> faithfulness in daily life and work,

1

marriage and family life,
the young and the elderly,
those engaged in education and in farming,
the hungry and the unemployed,
the sick and the dying,
national and international relations,
peace and justice,
nuclear peril and Christian hope.

Only when the net is cast as widely as this does the wideness of God's mercy become in practical terms as well as in liturgical settings the one sufficient foundation on which to build the Church's prayer and life.

The use to which these litanies are put in worship will vary from tradition to tradition. Certain of them can be employed as the "Prayers of the People," serving as the climax of the Liturgy of the Word after the Gospel has been read, preached and affirmed. In non-eucharistic settings they can be used in place of the minister's pastoral prayer or at the close of a morning or evening office. Carefully chosen, one of the litanies could be an appropriate congregational response to a sermon preached on a particular text or theme. Some clearly belong in services focused on such concerns as the mission of the Church, the peace of the world, the nurture of the young, or the care of the elderly. Others could well be sung; no pieces of paper would be required since the same refrain is repeated throughout the litany and thus is readily learned and used (the chief reason for the popularity of litanies in the past). In the case of litanies employing more than one voice or the successive stanzas of a hymn, careful preparation is obviously called for.

In any event, each occasion of public worship should allow for an *ample* time of common prayer for others. Without doing violence to the tradition of a particular church or the structure of a given liturgical rite, it is certainly possible to make use of the litany form of prayer week by week or from time to time. As in every other aspect of liturgical planning and leadership, pastoral sensitivity and imagination are needed if these litanies are to be grafted faithfully and with integrity into the worship of a particular community of faith.

The most helpful demonstration of how this book can be used with pastoral sensitivity and imagination is to let the litanies speak for themselves. Each of the examples cited below will indicate ways in which that particular litany and others like it may serve to enlarge the Church's prayer.

2

Litany 9:   *Adapting to a Particular Tradition*
                 This litany demonstrates the need for care and
                 forethought in using material which is obviously
                 derived from and speaks to one particular tradition or
                 denomination. The "diocese" has its equivalent in
                 synods, presbyteries and conferences. As a result this
                 litany, like others in this collection, can be
                 imaginatively adapted to the needs of other traditions
                 and situations. They cannot be taken over uncritically,
                 but neither should they be abandoned because at first
                 glance they seem to belong elsewhere in the Christian
                 household!

Litany 15:   *Regular Intercession*
                 Writing to the Christian community in Rome, St. Paul
                 says, "Never flag in zeal, be aglow with the Spirit
                 . . . rejoice in your hope . . . be constant in prayer
                 (Romans 12:11-12). Litany 15 is in fact a seven-part
                 cycle of intercessions for the mission of the Church,
                 and it would be most effective if used day in and day
                 out on a regular basis. Perhaps different groups or
                 individuals could observe different days in the cycle,
                 while the whole congregation shared in the seven
                 parts of the litany on seven successive Sundays. What
                 matters is that the Church's calling to pray for the
                 world be commended and implemented in a sustained
                 rather than a sporadic manner.

Litany 17:   *Sung Prayer*
                 Traditionally, litanies were meant to be sung, and this
                 fact draws attention to the role of the trained church
                 musician. In many churches the minister of music is
                 entirely capable of writing musical settings for some
                 of the litanies in this collection. The capacities of
                 leader, choir and congregation should be borne in
                 mind, and some time devoted to teaching the people
                 their response(s). Once the congregation is assured
                 and can play a full part in the singing of this litany, it
                 could well be sung in procession on an appropriate
                 occasion.

Litany 23:	*Long Litanies*

This is a lengthy litany which could not readily be used in a shortened form. However, there is much to be said for using it when there is ample time for lifting up the whole sweep of the Christian life faithfully lived. In the same way, Litany 119 calls for sufficient time to ponder and pray about the as yet unfulfilled aspirations contained in the Universal Declaration of Human Rights.

Litany 28:	*Dependence on Scripture*

The manifold references to Scripture have been deliberately reproduced in this litany in order to show the author's imaginative and faithful use of the New Testament. Indeed, Lucien Deiss originally called his book *Prières Bibliques* (Biblical Prayers). This particular litany may well inspire others to obey the Gospel injunction: "Go and do likewise."

Litany 63:	*Silence*

The restoration of the "Prayers of the People" requires that silent prayer on the part of the whole congregation be taken with great seriousness and that ample time be allowed for it between the biddings or petitions. Instruction on the creative use of silence for corporate prayer of this kind may well be needed. What matters is that neither leader nor congregation be intimidated by sustained periods of silence. Those fearful of silence will inevitably be tempted to curtail it or to fill it needlessly with yet more words.

Times of silence can also be introduced into many of the litanies in this collection, even if no formal provision is made for them in the text. For instance, silence would be effective in Litany 93 after every use of the word "evil" by the congregation. It would allow the sobering contents of the litany to be more fully appropriated, and this would also be true in the case of Litanies 6 and 96.

Litany 66:	*Appropriate Leadership*

The two leaders of this litany should certainly be young people, just as an older member of the community or congregation should lead Litany 60. However, in view of its contents, Litany 92 *(For the Elderly)* should certainly *not* be led by an older person.

Litany 115 would be strikingly effective if the different voices belonged to people whose homes were in the several continents mentioned in the course of the prayer.

Litany 76: *Archaic Language*
Although most of the ancient litanies are to be found in Volume One, this particular litany has a quaintness of language which may commend it to some, while disconcerting others. It has been discreetly modernized here in order to allow a fine and imaginative prayer from the seventeenth century to be used in our day by people whose fundamental needs and concerns are not markedly different from those of Bishop Andrewes.

Litany 79: *Hymn Stanzas as Part of a Litany*
One effective way of helping people to sing parts of a litany is illustrated here. The tune must be familiar if congregational participation is to be strong and confident. Many such combinations are possible; for example, Litany 121, which is meant to be recited on Memorial Day, could well be matched with Rosamond Herklots' hymn, "Forgive our sins as we forgive" (set to the tune *Detroit* in the *Lutheran Book of Worship*). Similarly, Litany 103 or Litany 104 would be wonderfully enriched if used with F. Pratt Green's hymn, "O Christ, the Healer, we have come." This text may be sung to another early American tune, *Distress,* to which it is set in the *Lutheran Book of Worship.* However, more familiar tunes in the appropriate meter can readily be substituted for *Detroit* (Common Meter) or *Distress* (Long Meter).

Litany 82: *Particular Intentions*
As an alternative to intercessions freely interpolated into an otherwise formal litany, the leader may mention at the start various concerns or persons in order that the congregation may bear them in mind during the ensuing litany. This is yet another way of ensuring that a general prayer is firmly rooted in specific lives and needs. Since this particular litany is intended for use in a context either of national celebration or of national crisis, there should be obvious intentions to commend to the congregation's prayers.

Litany 101:   *Controversial Content*
This litany should certainly be used but needs to be preceded by teaching or preaching which would indicate its thoroughly Biblical basis. Without that preparation it may serve only to divide, and in that way people may be wrongly spared the "hard sayings" which are the rough edges of the Gospel proclaimed and lived by Jesus Christ.

Litany 105:   *Free Intercessions*
During the two periods of silence in this litany the congregation could well be invited to add their own thanksgivings. During the first silence specific individuals could be mentioned, while at the end of the litany general categories could be added if they have not already been mentioned in the course of the litany. In Litany 89 the leader or the presiding minister could invite those present to add to the already extensive and impressionistic list of reasons for thankfulness. Since most people are reluctant to voice their gratitude to God in the context of public worship, it would be good to encourage adults as much as young people to contribute freely to the praying of this litany of thanksgiving.

Ample time is again the secret of success, together with instruction, encouragement and some attention to the question of audibility, especially in a large space or a numerous company. As in the case of silence, spontaneous contributions to a litany of this kind will increase as people become familiar and comfortable with an as yet novel form of corporate prayer.

Litany 126:   *Careful Preparation*
As with Litany 101, this litany requires that great care be taken to prepare the congregation to enter into covenant together. There is a danger inherent in reading words off a page or out of a book without weighing either the content or the consequences. To make a covenant in God's name, as John Wesley certainly appreciated, is a most solemn undertaking which asks of all who participate in it both prayerful preparation and honest self-examination. That should be true of all prayer, but certainly true of a litany such as this.

The litanies mentioned above, indeed all the litanies in this collection, are meant to be models or patterns which will inspire leaders of worship to use this form of prayer imaginatively in the regular worship of their respective congregations. The book is, of course, also a resource to be drawn upon by those who take seriously the desire and hope expressed by the Second Vatican Council: "that all the faithful should be led to that full, conscious, and active participation in liturgical celebrations which is demanded by the very nature of the liturgy" *(Constitution on the Sacred Liturgy,* para. 14).

One further aspect of this book calls for comment. It will quickly become obvious that no indication is given of the changes which have been made in the various litanies. Since this is not an Oxford Book of Litanies, but an ecumenical collection intended for widespread use in worship at the end of the twentieth century, a great many alterations have proved necessary. These changes and adaptations will, in each case, have been made for one or more of the following reasons:

ecumenical applicability:	in order to extend the contents and appeal of a litany beyond the confines of a particular denomination;
inclusive language:	in order to avoid excessive use of such words as "men" or "mankind" which no longer convey the inclusive meaning they were certainly meant to convey when used in the litany in its original form;
contemporary references:	in order to broaden the categories mentioned in the various petitions of a litany and thereby to include more of life as we know it and live it in the closing years of this century;
intelligibility, brevity, and recitability:	in order to take into account the ways people pray in our day, the words they use, and the more concise forms of speech which are common to us;
inclusion of hymn stanzas:	in order to provide sung responses for use in liturgical settings where the traditional "sung litany" would not be familiar or acceptable;
division among several leaders:	in order to encourage greater diversity in the conduct and leadership of corporate prayer.

The classical form of the litany with its climax either in the Lord's Prayer or in a concluding collect said by the presiding minister has deliberately been avoided as an *invariable* model. This course has been followed for ecumenical and pastoral reasons, but those who wish to conclude a particular litany in either of these traditional ways may certainly do so.

A final word about leadership is in order. The person and presence of the leader are undoubtedly important. In an earlier and less ecumenical age the Puritans denounced the lifeless readings of collects from a book (in that instance the *Book of Common Prayer)* as "stinted prayer." The reading of litanies from *this* book can certainly fall prey to the same disease of lifelessness, and merit the same unpromising diagnosis! Careful preparation, sensitive adaptation, thoughtful integration with the other parts of the service, ample provision for silence or the free interpolation of additional petitions, unhurried pacing of the prayer, clear and audible reading, specificity without unnecessary divisiveness and generality without meaningless platitudes: these all are vital to the effective use of the litany as a form of corporate prayer. No leader is meant to pre-empt or stifle the priestly function of the people of God as they pray for the world. In like manner, no leader is meant to inhibit or cripple their prayer by poor and unthinking leadership.

In bringing this second volume of litanies to a close, I want to express yet again my gratitude to The Seabury Press and especially to my editors, Jack Whelan of the Seabury Press and more recently Hermann Weinlick of Winston Press. They have been at all times supportive and encouraging so that this enterprise, once begun, was continued until it was thoroughly finished.

I am once more conscious of the part that Victoria Strane has played in bringing this collection into being. The enthusiasm, insight and care she has brought to the readying of the manuscript are special gifts for which I am most thankful.

I am grateful also that I can dedicate this second volume to my parents who have always lived out their prayer more than they have spoken about it.

This collection of litanies is offered to those who will use it in that same spirit. It calls on God's mercy in all of its height and depth and length and breadth. The wideness of that mercy knows only the limits we impose on it in our lack of faith or hope or love. As Frederick William Faber wrote in 1862,

> "For the love of God is broader
> Than the measure of man's mind;
> And the heart of the Eternal
> Is most wonderfully kind."

What matters is that the Church pray and live with that assurance, for that is the best witness we can give to the world in the testing days ahead.

Yale and Berkeley Divinity Schools
New Haven, Connecticut   March 21, 1985

8

†††Prayer and
†††Mission

The Church

•1 For the Church of Christ

O Christ the Rock, on which your people, as living stones joined together, grow into a spiritual house;
Defend your Church, we pray.

O Christ the Vine, of which your people are the branches;
Defend your Church, we pray.

O Christ the Head of the Body, of which your people are the members;
Defend your Church, we pray.

O Christ our Prophet, you teach the way of God in truth;
Defend your Church, we pray.

O Christ our Priest, you offered yourself upon the Cross, and now make intercession for us to the Father;
Defend your Church, we pray.

O Christ our King, you reign over all the earth, and make us citizens of your heavenly kingdom;
Defend your Church, we pray.

O Christ, you sent the Holy Spirit upon the Church, clothing it with power from on high;
Defend your Church, we pray.

We pray to you, Lord Christ.
Lord, hear our prayer.

That we may be devoted to the Apostles' teaching and fellowship, to the breaking of bread and the prayers,
Lord, hear our prayer.

That we may make disciples of all nations, baptizing them in the Name of the Father, and of the Son, and of the Holy Spirit,

Lord, hear our prayer.

That you will fulfill your promise to be with us always, even to the ages of ages,
Lord, hear our prayer.

That you will sustain all members of your holy Church, that in our vocation and ministry we may truly and devoutly serve you,
Lord, hear our prayer.

That you will bless the clergy of your Church, that they may diligently preach the Gospel and faithfully celebrate the holy Sacraments,
Lord, hear our prayer.

That you will heal the divisions in your Church, that all may be one, even as you and the Father are one,
Lord, hear our prayer.

Arise, O God, maintain your cause;
Do not forget the lives of the poor.

Look down from heaven, behold and tend this vine;
Preserve what your right hand has planted.

Let your priests be clothed with righteousness;
Let your faithful people sing with joy.

The Lord be with you.
And also with you.

Let us pray.

(Silence)

Let your continual mercy cleanse and defend your Church, O Lord;
and, because we cannot continue in safety without your help,
protect and govern us always by your goodness;
through Jesus Christ our Lord,
who lives and reigns with you and the Holy Spirit,
one God, for ever and ever. Amen.

THE BOOK OF OCCASIONAL SERVICES

•2 The Work of the Church

O God the Father, who hast made of one blood all nations of the earth;
Have mercy upon us.

O God the Son, who hast redeemed the world from the power of darkness;
Have mercy upon us.

O God the Holy Ghost, by whom the whole body of the Church is governed and sanctified;
Have mercy upon us.

O Father, Son, and Holy Ghost, three Persons and one God, Creator, Redeemer, Sanctifier;
Have mercy upon us.

Our past unfaithfulness;
O Lord, forgive.

Our neglect of opportunities;
O Lord, forgive.

Our deafness to thy calls;
O Lord, forgive.

Our slothfulness and want of zeal;
O Lord, forgive.

By thy holy Incarnation;
Jesu, hear and save.

By thy call to thine apostles;
Jesu, hear and save.

By thy feeding of the multitudes;
Jesu, hear and save.

By thy sacrifice upon the cross;
Jesu, hear and save.

By thy heavenly intercession;
Jesu, hear and save.

By thine ever-abiding presence with thy Church;
Jesu, hear and save.

We sinners do beseech thee to hear us, that it may please thee to bless thy holy Church, which thou has purchased with thy most precious blood;
Hear us, we beseech thee.

That thou wouldest heal all dissensions among Christians, which hinder the spread of thy gospel;
Hear us, we beseech thee.

That thou wouldest fill the Church in every land with the spirit of love and prayer for those who know thee not;

Hear us, we beseech thee.

That thou wouldest increase the number of laborers in thy harvest, and grant them the abundance of thy blessing;
Hear us, we beseech thee.

For all ministers of the Gospel and for all Christ's faithful servants in every land (especially _____);
Hear us, we beseech thee.

That it may please thee to give them an earnest love of souls, wisdom to win them, diligence to keep them, and undying zeal for their perfection;
Hear us, we beseech thee.

That it may please thee to grant them the gift of languages for making known thy truth;
Hear us, we beseech thee.

That it may please thee to be their strength in sickness and danger, in discouragement and loneliness, and show them thy salvation;
Hear us, we beseech thee.

That it may please thee to confirm and strengthen with the fullness of thy grace all converts to the faith, giving them perseverance unto the end;
Hear us, we beseech thee.

That it may please thee to make fruitful for good the medical and educational missions of thy Church;
Hear us, we beseech thee.

That it may please thee to support and embolden, by the power of thy good Spirit, those who labor for the ignorant and oppressed;
Hear us, we beseech thee.

That it may please thee to break down everywhere the barriers of caste and color;
Hear us, we beseech thee.

That it may please thee to convert the heathen, leading them out of darkness and error and into the clear light and true knowledge of thee;
Hear us, we beseech thee.

That it may please thee to fulfill in Christ all the faiths and longings of the world;
Hear us, we beseech thee.

That it may please thee to bless and enrich the Church in every place, making it truly catholic in faith and love;
Hear us, we beseech thee.

That it may please thee to call all people to thyself and to hasten thy kingdom;
Hear us, we beseech thee.

O Savior of the world, who by thy cross and precious blood hast redeemed us;
Save us and help us, we humbly beseech thee, O Lord.

O God, who hast made of one blood all nations for to dwell on the face of the earth, and didst send thy blessed Son Jesus Christ to preach peace to them that are afar off, and to them that are nigh; Grant that all the peoples of the world may feel after thee and find thee; and hasten, O Lord, the fulfillment of thy promise, to pour out thy Spirit upon all flesh; through Jesus Christ our Lord.
Amen.

THE CUDDESDON COLLEGE OFFICE BOOK

•3 The Names of the Church

God of Abraham and Isaac, of apostles and prophets: in every age you have picked out people to work for you, by showing justice and doing mercy. Let the church share Christ's own work as prophet, priest, and king, reconciling the world to your law and your love, and telling your mighty power.

Give thanks to God for the church of Jesus Christ.
We are a chosen people.

You have called us out of the world, O God, and chosen us to be a witness to nations. Give us your Spirit to show the way, the truth, and the life of our Savior Jesus Christ.
Forgive silence and stubbornness. Help us to be your chosen people.

Give thanks to God for the church of Jesus Christ.
We are a royal priesthood.

You have appointed us priests, O God, to pray for people everywhere and to declare your mercy. Give us your Spirit; that, sacrificing ourselves for neighbors in love, they may be drawn to you, and to each other.
Forgive hypocrisy and lazy prayers. Help us to be your royal priesthood.

Give thanks to God for the church of Jesus Christ.
We are the household of God.

You have baptized us into one family of faith, and named us your children, the sisters and brothers of Christ. Give us your Spirit to live in peace and serve each other gladly.
Forgive pride and unloving divisions. Help us to be your household.

Give thanks to God for the church of Jesus Christ.
We are a temple for your Spirit.

You have built us up, O God, into a temple for worship. Give us your Spirit to know there is no other foundation for us than Jesus Christ, rock and redeemer.
Forgive weakness and lack of reverence. Help us to be a temple for your Spirit.

Give thanks to God for the church of Jesus Christ.
We are a colony of heaven.

You have welcomed us as your citizens, O God, to represent our homeland here on earth. Give us your Spirit to do your will, speak your language, and to show by our style of life your kingdom's courtesy and love.
Forgive injustice and going along with the world. Help us to be a colony of heaven.

Give thanks to God for the church of Jesus Christ.
We are the body of Christ.

You have joined us in one body, O God, to live for our Lord in the world. Give us your Spirit; that, working together without envy or pride, we may serve our Lord and Head.
Forgive slack faith and separate ways. Help us to be the body of Christ.

O God, we are your church, called, adopted, built up, blessed, and joined to Jesus Christ. Help us to know who we are, and in all we do to be your useful servants.

We are a chosen people
  a royal priesthood
  a household of God
  a temple for the Spirit
  a colony of heaven
  the body of Christ

Give thanks to God,
For the church of Jesus Christ.

Give thanks to God,
And trust the Holy Spirit. Amen.

THE WORSHIPBOOK

•4 Our Forebears in the Faith

Almighty God: you built your church on the rock of human faith and trust; we praise you for Jesus Christ, the foundation and cornerstone of all we believe.
We praise you, God.

For Abraham, Isaac, and Jacob; for Sarah, Rebekah and Rachel; and for Moses, who led your people out of slavery and established the law in their hearts;
We praise you, God.

For the prophets who listened for your word and called your people back from disobedience and from the worship of man-made gods;
We praise you, God.

For those who foretold the coming of your Son Jesus Christ, and prepared the way for his birth;
We praise you, God.

For Mary and Joseph, who taught him to love you and trained him in synagogue and temple to serve you;
We praise you, God.

For Christ, our Savior, who loved us and gave himself for us on the cross;
We praise you, God.

For the apostles and martyrs of the church, who gave their lives that we, in our day, might receive the good news of grace and forgiveness;
We praise you, God.

For the great men and women of every age, whose love for your church made it a willing instrument of your care and mercy; who placed you first in their lives and held to their faith in good times and in bad;
We praise you, God, through Jesus Christ our Lord. Amen.

THE WORSHIPBOOK

•5 For Faithfulness in Our Day

Save us, Father, from living in the past, and from resting on the work of others. Let us find a new beginning and a new vision; that we may know our duty in this place and this world today.
O Lord, hear us.

Keep us from pride that excludes others from the shelter of your love; and from mean prejudice and mass evils that scar the tissues of our common life.
O Lord, hear us.

Spare us from the selfishness that uses your house as a means of getting social position or personal glory, and let us not hold back what we have or what we are when there is so much need.
O Lord, hear us.

Defend us from the ignorance that nourishes injustice and from indifference that causes hearts to break; that, in these times of racial bitterness, we may demonstrate your love and live beyond caste or color as Christ's men and women.
O Lord, hear us.

Help us to avoid isolation in our apartments and our private homes, while others near us do not have a bed of their own or any quiet place; and, as we work to bring a decent life to others, let us know a purer enjoyment of all your blessing.
O Lord, hear us, for we pray in Jesus' name. Amen.

THE WORSHIPBOOK

•6 A Litany of Modern Myths

Leader 1: St. Paul wrote to Timothy, "The time is coming when people will not endure sound teaching, but having itching ears will gather for themselves teachers to suit their own fancy. They will turn away from listening to the truth and wander into myths." His advice to Timothy was this: "For your part, stand by the truths you have learned and are assured of."

(II Timothy 3:14; 4:3-4)

(Silence)

Leader 2: Modern thought is superior to all past forms of understanding reality and is therefore normative for Christian faith and life.

All: *"For your part, stand by the truths you have learned and are assured of."*

Leader 1: Religious statements are totally independent of reasonable discourse.

All: *"For your part, stand by the truths you have learned and are assured of."*

Leader 2: Religious language refers to human experience and nothing else, God being humanity's noblest creation.

All: *"For your part, stand by the truths you have learned and are assured of."*

Leader 1: Jesus can only be understood in terms of contemporary models of humanity.

All: *"For your part, stand by the truths you have learned and are assured of."*

Leader 2: All religions are equally valid; the choice among them is not a matter of conviction about truth but only of personal preference or life-style.

All: *"For your part, stand by the truths you have learned and are assured of."*

Leader 1: To realize one's true potential and to be true to oneself is the whole meaning of salvation.

All: *"For your part, stand by the truths you have learned and are assured of."*

Leader 2: Since what is human is good, evil can adequately be understood as failure to realize human potential.

All: *"For your part, stand by the truths you have learned and are assured of."*

Leader 1: The sole purpose of worship is to promote individual self-realization and human community.

All: *"For your part, stand by the truths you have learned and are assured of."*

Leader 2: Institutions and historical traditions are oppressive and inimical to our being truly human; liberation from them is required for authentic existence and authentic religion.

All: *"For your part, stand by the truths you have learned and are assured of."*

Leader 1: The world must set the agenda for the Church. Social, political and economic programs to improve the quality of life are ultimately normative for the Church's mission in the world.

| *All:* | *"For your part, stand by the truths you have learned and are assured of."* |

| Leader 2: | An emphasis on God's transcendence is at least a hindrance to, and perhaps incompatible with, Christian social concern and action. |

| *All:* | *"For your part, stand by the truths you have learned and are assured of."* |

| Leader 1: | The struggle for a better humanity will bring about the Kingdom of God. |

| *All:* | *"For your part, stand by the truths you have learned and are assured of."* |

| Leader 2: | The question of hope beyond death is irrelevant or at best marginal to the Christian understanding of human fulfillment. |

| *All:* | *"For your part, stand by the truths you have learned and are assured of."* |

Almighty God, whom truly to know is everlasting life: Grant us so perfectly to know your Son Jesus Christ to be the way, the truth, and the life, that we may steadfastly follow his steps in the way that leads to eternal life; through Jesus Christ your Son our Lord, who lives and reigns with you, in the unity of the Holy Spirit, one God, for ever and ever. Amen.

BASED ON "THE HARTFORD APPEAL FOR THEOLOGICAL AFFIRMATION"*

*Where an asterisk occurs at the end of a litany, this indicates that additional information may be found in the *Notes* which follow Litany 127.

•7 For the Renewal of the Church

Let us pray to the Lord and Giver of life that the Church of God may be renewed and strengthened for its mission in our day.

(Silence)

That the Church may become alive again with the fire of her first charity, fearless of danger and reckless unto death, in the splendor of that Life which is the light of the world.
Holy Spirit, hear us.

That she may be worthy of her liberty, persistent in reform, active in benevolence, trusting the people, and ever faithful to the Jerusalem which is above, and free, and the mother of us all,
Holy Spirit, hear us.

That her old may dream dreams, and her young see visions; that her sons and her daughters may prophesy, bearing eager witness of her beauty to the world,
Holy Spirit, hear us.

That all her members, putting self aside, disinterested and pure in heart, may seek and find God, and rejoice in the truth,
Holy Spirit, hear us.

That her ministers may be good and wise, strong and very courageous, competent in their work, and faithful in their witness,
Holy Spirit, hear us.

That her bishops, full of insight and imagination, may venture great things, not exercising dominion, but serving as true leaders of the people,
Holy Spirit, hear us.

That her councils and conventions may be keen to go forward, filled with wisdom, eager to rebuild the walls of Jerusalem,
Holy Spirit, hear us.

That her scholars may have disciples, her prophets hearers, her saints imitators, and all her pioneers many anxious to follow in their steps,
Holy Spirit, hear us.

That we may forsake that love of party which keeps us from loving one another; and so, coming together in friendship, we may find the overpowering love of God, which shall knit us all together in one united Church,
Holy Spirit, hear us.

And, finally, that the Church, with love recovered in her midst, may teach all to love one another, and all nations to dwell together in helpfulness and friendship, reconciled and redeemed,
Holy Spirit, hear us.

Father, be with us all.
Christ, be with us all.
Holy Spirit, be with us all.
Be with us, Holy God, now and evermore.

God, our Shepherd, give to the Church a new vision and a new charity, new wisdom and fresh understanding, the revival of her brightness and the renewal of her unity; that the eternal message of your Son may be hailed as the good news of the new age; through him who makes all things new, even Jesus Christ our Lord.
Amen.

THE KINGDOM, THE POWER AND THE GLORY

•8 For All Manner of Churches

Lord Jesus, Head of the Church, your Body:
We thank you for your ecumenical Church –
suffering, militant, and triumphant at the last.

We thank you for powerhouses of spiritual energy within your Church: for Catholic retreat centers, Orthodox monasteries, and evangelical communities like Iona in Scotland and Taizé in France.
Help them by their example to put energy and spirit
into our witness also.

We thank you for rural churches, serving farming communities and providing much strength for those on whom we all depend.
Help them to find new ways of joint service
and to avoid the pitfall of self-pity.

We thank you for churches in small towns, focal points in their peoples' striving for the enhancement of their common life.
Help them to keep in touch with the problems and needs of your world,
reaching out with a will to learn and to love.

We thank you for churches in commuter suburbs: for their ministry to whole families and for their deep interest in family wholeness.
Help them to avoid the illusion of independence and of self-sufficiency
and remind them of their mission to the cities.

Lord, we thank you for city churches, fighting for their life, and making the changes necessary to work with new people, people moving in and moving out, all your children, all loved by you.
Help such churches to be versatile,
adaptable, imaginative, resourceful.

We thank you for specialized churches, experimental churches, churches where Christians unlike us, who feel unaccepted by us or who cannot themselves accept us, are seeking you.
Help them to find you, and strip us and them of truculence and hate,
that we may find each other in you.

We thank you for churches which do not seem like churches at all: for Christians meeting for Bible study in a living room, Christians gathering secretly to celebrate the Eucharist, Christians meeting at great peril to themselves in many parts of your world.
Help them to be aware of the world-wide communion
of Christians who care for them and pray for them always.

Lord Jesus, Head of the Church, your Body:
We thank you for your ecumenical Church,
suffering, militant, and triumphant at the last. Amen.

MODELS FOR MINISTERS I*

•9 For the Diocese

Let us pray for the Church in this diocese.

We beseech thee to pour thine abundant blessing upon thy Servant *N.* _____, Bishop of this diocese; and that *he* may be guided and guarded day by day in leading and serving those who are committed to *his* charge:
We beseech thee to hear us, good Lord.

That it may please thee to bless the Cathedral of _____ in _____, and so to shed thy grace upon the Dean and Chapter, and all its staff, that they may make it a true mother church of the diocese;
We beseech thee to hear us, good Lord.

That it may please thee to direct the hearts and minds of all who assist the Bishop in the administration of this diocese;
We beseech thee to hear us, good Lord.

That it may please thee to bless all the Clergy of the diocese, that they may be faithful stewards of thy mysteries, and set forward the salvation of people everywhere;

We beseech thee to hear us, good Lord.

That it may please thee to grant thine abundant blessing to all called to labor in our cities, that they may pursue their task with steadfastness and love;
We beseech thee to hear us, good Lord.

That it may please thee to bless all who work in the small towns and villages of the diocese, that they may be sustained and directed in the special circumstances of their life and ministry;
We beseech thee to hear us, good Lord.

That it may please thee to call to the work of the ministry men and women who are full of the Holy Ghost and of faith, and to endue them with the spirit of power, and of love, and of a sound mind;
We beseech thee to hear us, good Lord.

That it may please thee to bless all those who are engaged in training candidates for the ministry in universities, seminaries and divinity schools;
We beseech thee to hear us, good Lord.

That it may please thee to sanctify the lives and work of those who exercise the ministry of Lay Reader, that the worship of the Church may be maintained, and thy people edified;
We beseech thee to hear us, good Lord.

That it may please thee to guide and uphold Lay Missioners, and all who are especially engaged in the work of evangelism;
We beseech thee to hear us, good Lord.

That it may please thee to grant to all Churchwardens and Vestry members grace to execute their trust with loyalty and devotion;
We beseech thee to hear us, good Lord.

That it may please thee to inspire all Choristers, Choirmasters, and Organists, that they may lead the praises of thy people with understanding;
We beseech thee to hear us, good Lord.

That it may please thee to prosper the work of all who teach and learn in our Sunday Schools; that our children may grow up in thy faith and fear, and in the knowledge and love of Christ;
We beseech thee to hear us, good Lord.

That it may please thee to bless those who work in the Diocesan Offices, and to grant that they may ever be conscious of serving Christ in serving his Church;
We beseech thee to hear us, good Lord.

That it may please thee to guide those who are responsible for the management of the Diocesan Conference Center(s) at _____, that *it* may minister to the needs of Clergy and Laity alike;
We beseech thee to hear us, good Lord.

That it may please thee to fill with thy spirit all who serve on our diocesan councils and committees, that they may ever seek the advancement of thy kingdom and have a right judgment in all things;
We beseech thee to hear us, good Lord.

That it may please thee to bless all religious communities, that by their life and prayers, and understanding of thy word, they may strengthen and enrich thy Church;
We beseech thee to hear us, good Lord.

That it may please thee to bless all societies and guilds in the diocese, especially _____, that every member of the same may be strong to bear witness to the truth with faith and courage;
We beseech thee to hear us, good Lord.

That it may please thee to give us a more earnest spirit of prayer, almsgiving, and self-denial, that those who know thee not may be brought to share the blessings which we so richly enjoy;
We beseech thee to hear us, good Lord.

That it may please thee to move the hearts of thy people to give of themselves and of their substance willingly and regularly for the work of the Church, especially _____, that progress be not hindered nor opportunity fail;
We beseech thee to hear us, good Lord.

That it may please thee to grant that our work for the Church at home may be matched by a greater zeal for the extension of thy kingdom overseas;
We beseech thee to hear us, good Lord.

O Savior of the world, who by thy Cross and precious Blood hast redeemed us:
Save us, and help us, we humbly beseech thee, O Lord.

Let us pray.
Lord, have mercy upon us.
Christ, have mercy upon us.
Lord, have mercy upon us.

Our Father, who art in heaven,
   hallowed be thy Name,
   thy kingdom come,
   thy will be done,
      on earth as it is in heaven.

Give us this day our daily bread.
And forgive us our trespasses,
   as we forgive those who trespass against us.
And lead us not into temptation,
   but deliver us from evil.
For thine is the kingdom, and the power, and the glory,
   for ever and ever. Amen.

EMBER PRAYERS

•10 For the Welfare of the Church

That it may please thee to strengthen and enlarge thy holy Church in every land, and to unite all those who profess and call themselves Christians,
We beseech thee, good Lord.

That thy Church may strive not for its own safety, but for the world's salvation,
We beseech thee, good Lord.

That thy Church may proclaim the gospel throughout the whole earth,
We beseech thee, good Lord.

That thou wilt grant to all ministers of thy word and sacraments the spirit of wisdom, power, and love,
We beseech thee, good Lord.

That thou wilt give to all thy people grace to understand and believe thy word, and to show forth their faith in their lives,
We beseech thee, good Lord.

That thou wilt remove from us all hatred, prejudice, and narrowness of thought, so that we may rejoice in all that thou dost reveal,
We beseech thee, good Lord.

That thou wilt so guide us in all perplexities of belief and conduct, that we may hold fast that which is true, and faithfully confess thee before the world,
We beseech thee, good Lord.

That regardless of the praise or contempt of the world, thy Church may worship thee in spirit and in truth,
We beseech thee, good Lord.

And as we pray for the Church universal, so let us pray for God's blessing on the Church in this place.

Here may the faithful find salvation, and the careless be awakened.

Amen.

Here may the tempted find help, and the sorrowful comfort.
Amen.

Here may the weary find rest, and the strong be renewed.
Amen.

Here may the aged find peace, and the young be inspired.
Amen.

Now unto God that is able to do exceeding abundantly above all that we ask or think,
According to the power that worketh in us,
Unto God be glory in the Church and in Christ Jesus unto all generations for ever and ever. *Amen.*

PRAYERS FOR A NEW WORLD

•11 For Ourselves

That we may accept the responsibility of our freedom, the burden of our privilege, and so conduct ourselves as to set an example for those who will follow after;
O God, be our strength.

That we may not be content with a secondhand faith, worshiping words rather than the Word;
O God, be our strength.

That we may find joy in the study of Scripture, and growth in exposure to new ideas;
O God, be our strength.

That we may be part of our local fellowship of churches and our community, sharing in the great mission which you have set before us, and always seeking the common good;
O God, be our strength.

That we may find in your church a prod to our imaginations, a shock to our laziness, and a source of power to do your will;
O God, be our strength.

O God, who gave us minds to know you, hearts to love you, and voices to sing your praise: send your Spirit among us; that, confronted by your truth, we may be free to worship you as we should; through Jesus Christ our Lord.
Amen.

THE WORSHIPBOOK

•12 Litany of Jesus Praying

Father, the hour is come; glorify thy Son, that thy Son may glorify thee.
Father in heaven;
Hallowed be thy name.

As thou hast given him power over all flesh, that he might give eternal life
to all whom thou hast given him,
Father in heaven;
Hallowed be thy name.

And this is life eternal, that they should know thee, the only true God, and
Jesus Christ whom thou has sent.
Father in heaven;
Hallowed be thy name.

I have glorified thee on the earth; I have finished the work that thou gavest
me to do.
Father in heaven;
Hallowed be thy name.

And now, Father, glorify thou me with thine own self, with the glory which I
had with thee before the world was.
Father in heaven;
Hallowed be thy name.

I have manifested thy Name unto those whom thou gavest me out of the
world.
Father in heaven;
Thy kingdom come.

I pray for them; I pray not for the world but for those whom thou hast given
me, for they are thine.
Father in heaven;
Thy kingdom come.

Holy Father, keep in thy Name those whom thou hast given me, that they
may be one, even as we are one.
Father in heaven;
Thy kingdom come.

These things I speak in the world, that they may have my joy fulfilled in
themselves.
Father in heaven;
Thy kingdom come.

I have given them thy word; and the world hath hated them because they are
not of the world, even as I am not of the world.

Father in heaven;
Thy kingdom come.

I pray not that thou shouldest take them out of the world, but that thou shouldest keep them from the evil one.
Father in heaven;
Thy will be done.

They are not of the world, even as I am not of the world.
Father in heaven;
Thy will be done.

Sanctify them in the truth; thy word is truth.
Father in heaven;
Thy will be done.

As thou hast sent me into the world, even so have I sent them into the world.
Father in heaven;
Thy will be done.

And for their sakes I sanctify myself, that they also may be sanctified in the truth.
Father in heaven;
Thy will be done.

Neither do I pray for these alone, but for them also who shall believe on me through their word.
Father in heaven;
Thy will be done.

That they all may be one, as thou, Father, art in me, and I in thee.
Father in heaven;
Thy will be done.

That they also may be one in us, that the world may believe that thou hast sent me.
Father in heaven;
Thy will be done.

And the glory which thou gavest me have I given them, that they may be one even as we are one.
Father in heaven;
Thy will be done.

I in them and thou in me, that they may be perfected into one.
Father in heaven;
Thy will be done.

That the world may know that thou hast sent me and has loved them as thou hast loved me.
Father in heaven;
Thy will be done.

Our Father, who art in heaven, Hallowed be thy Name; Thy kingdom come; Thy will be done; On earth as it is in heaven. Give us this day our daily bread. And forgive us our trespasses, As we forgive those who trespass against us. And lead us not into temptation; But deliver us from evil.

Father, I will that they also, whom thou hast given me, be with me where I am, that they may behold my glory which thou hast given me.
For thine is the kingdom, the power, and the glory, for ever and ever.

For thou lovedst me before the foundation of the world.
For thine is the kingdom, the power, and the glory, for ever and ever.

O righteous Father, the world hath not known thee, but I have known thee; and these have known that thou hast sent me.
For thine is the kingdom, the power, and the glory, for ever and ever.

And I have made known unto them thy Name, and will make it known, that the love with which thou hast loved me may be in them, and I in them.
For thine is the kingdom, the power, and the glory, for ever and ever. Amen.

THE ANGLICAN BENEDICTINES OF NASHDOM ABBEY
–EMBER PRAYERS

• 13 Dedication to God's Design

Let us kneel and offer ourselves to God that we may know how to take our share in God's design for the world.

Let us pray.

(Silence)

That we may put ourselves alongside our fellows and see the Christian faith and life from their point of view:
Lord, hear our prayer.

That the Church may be aware of the rapid rate of change both in the thought of men and women and in their social circumstances:
Lord, hear our prayer.

For the wisdom of the Holy Spirit in the large-scale and complex problems of society and work today, which require corporate judgments and solutions:
Lord, hear our prayer.

That in the choices facing us today in situations partly good and partly evil, we may be granted the insights of the Holy Spirit, and guided to make decisions which will forward your will:
Lord, hear our prayer.

That you will grant to Christians working in big organizations the faith to share in some small way your active concern for the good ordering of people's lives and the supplying of their needs:
Lord, hear our prayer.

That we may see in our daily work the opportunity to serve you through the truth of our insights, the honesty of our service, and our concern for our fellow-workers:
Lord, hear our prayer.

That you will bless those groups of Christians who are trying to discover how they may best exercise Christian vocation through their professions:
Lord, hear our prayer.

That our local churches may no longer be seen as arks of safety, but as powerhouses of grace for the invading forces of your Kingdom:
Lord, hear our prayer.

That you will bless and guide all lay movements which seek to advance your Kingdom in special spheres of work or in particular neighborhoods:
Lord, hear our prayer.

That you will guide our local churches to face the challenge of these movements, to learn from them and to offer them understanding and grateful fellowship:
Lord, hear our prayer.

That you will enable the clergy to bring the light of your truth to your people and the grace of the sacraments to their strengthening:
Lord, hear our prayer.
Amen.

PRAYERS FOR TODAY'S CHURCH

• 14 All Christians in Their Vocation and Ministry

O Father, Creator, from whom the whole family in heaven and earth is named,
Have mercy on us.

O Son, Redeemer, through whom the world is reconciled to the Father,
Have mercy on us.

O Holy Spirit, Sanctifier, whose glory fills the world and searches the deep things of God,
Have mercy on us.

O Holy, blessed, and glorious Trinity, one God,
Have mercy on us.

From blind hearts and petty spirits, that refuse to see the need that all have for your love,
Good Lord, deliver us.

From pride, self-sufficiency, and the unwillingness to admit our need of your compassion,
Good Lord, deliver us.

From discouragement in the face of pain and disappointment, and from lack of persistence and thoroughness,
Good Lord, deliver us.

By your baptism into the sins of the world,
Good Lord, forgive us.

By your abundant feeding of the multitudes,
Good Lord, nourish us.

By your suffering and death, which breaks down every dividing wall of hostility,
Good Lord, reconcile us.

By your glorious resurrection and ascension,
Good Lord, renew us.

By your commission to the Apostles,
Good Lord, send us forth.

By the coming of the Holy Spirit, who unites all things in heaven and earth,
Good Lord, make us one.

Strengthen and encourage all who do your work in lonely and dangerous places.
Hear us, good Lord.

Open the hearts and hands of many for the support of your Church in every place.
Hear us, good Lord.

Touch our eyes, that we may see the glory of God in all creation.
Hear us, good Lord.

Touch our ears, that we may hear from every mouth the wonderful works of God.
Hear us, good Lord.

Touch our lips, that we may tell in every tongue the wonderful works of God.
Hear us, good Lord.

Touch our hands, that we may do the truth which you have taught us.
Hear us, good Lord.

Touch our feet, that we may go for you into all parts of the world.
Hear us, good Lord.

Our Father, who art in heaven,
hallowed be thy Name,
thy kingdom come,
thy will be done,
on earth as it is in heaven.
Give us this day our daily bread.
And forgive us our trespasses,
as we forgive those who trespass against us.
And lead us not into temptation,
but deliver us from evil.
For thine is the kingdom, and the power, and the glory,
for ever and ever. Amen.

(Concluding Collect)

O God, without whom our labor is in vain, and with whom the least of your children go forth as the mighty: Prosper all work undertaken according to your will; and grant to all whom you send a pure intention, patient faith, sufficient success upon earth, and the blessedness of serving you in heaven; through Jesus Christ our Lord.
Amen.

PRAYERS, THANKSGIVINGS, LITANIES

•15 A Cycle of Intercessions for the Mission of the Church

These litanies may be used separately or as a cycle of prayer on the seven days of the week.

Monday

Almighty Father, you give us life
as you give life to all people.
You call us into the Church
that with men and women
of different race, color, and language,
different experience and different traditions,
we may be one body
to the glory of Christ on earth.
Help us to be what you have called us to be.

You are the giver of life.
Father, renew us by your Spirit.

Father of all, you give us
wealth in the earth and in the oceans,
forests and fertile plains,
air to breathe, water to drink,
and all that is needful for human life.
We pray for those who know little of your bounty,
for whom the earth is a cruel desert
and existence a constant struggle
against overwhelming odds.
We acknowledge that their burdens should be our burdens;
we acknowledge that we share a common humanity.

You are the giver of life.
Father, renew us by your Spirit.

Father, you have so made us that we need one another,
but because we do not know how to love everyone,
you tell us to start with the sister or brother at our side.
We pray for any from whom we are estranged. Bless them,
and bless us in our future relationships with them.
We pray for our families, our friends,
and all whom we meet day by day . . .
In their particular needs we ask you to bless them.

You are the giver of life.

Father, renew us by your Spirit.

Father, you are present in every part of human experience.
We hold before you
the infant lying in a mother's arms,
the young lovers planning together their first home,
the sick and infirm battling with weakness and incapacity,
the dying, soon to experience your new creation.

You are the giver of life.
Father, renew us by your Spirit.

Eternal Father, we remember before you
those who have passed from this world . . .
As we all received from you the gift of life
so we pray that you will bring us to the life eternal.

You are the giver of life.
Father, renew us by your Spirit.
Amen.

Tuesday

We pray for the Church,
where all too often, like Cain,
we have made the worship offered by our brother
a cause for hostility and division.
We pray that our Lord may bind us together,
teaching us to value the richness of our diversity
and to rejoice in every fresh glimpse of God's glory
seen through traditions other than our own.

Lord, teach us to love:
That we may be children of God.

We pray for those lands where brother and sister fight sister and brother,
divided by arbitrary borders, ideology or religion.
We pray for those lands where extremes of wealth and poverty
are bitterly divisive.
We pray for those lands where power is grossly abused
and the dispossessed bear the heaviest burden.

Lord, teach us to love:
That we may be children of God.

We pray for all who have been nourished on bitterness

and fed with the wrongs suffered by earlier generations.
We pray for all who have grown to hate people
instead of hating that which evil has done to people.
We pray for the young who are impatient for change
and the not so young who resist all change.

Lord, teach us to love:
That we may be children of God.

We commend to God any special needs known to us . . .
As we remember the sick, the sorrowful, and all who are in any distress,
let us also remember that God has supremely made himself known to us as Savior
and calls us to share in God's rescuing work.

Lord, teach us to love:
That we may be children of God.

Lord, we would heal and not destroy.
Teach us the discipline of obedience to the commandment
"You shall love your neighbor as yourself,"
and give us the fortitude to go on obeying to the end.

Lord, teach us to love:
That we may be children of God.

Let us remember before God those who have died . . .
Lord we are all sinners and utterly dependent on your grace.
We praise you for the forgiveness of sins
by which men and women are enabled
to rise from death to eternal life.

Lord, teach us to love:
That we may be children of God.
Amen.

Wednesday

Lord Jesus, you have faced temptation,
you know how difficult it can be
to distinguish between vision and mirage,
between truth and falsehood.

Lord, help us when we are tempted:
And save us when we fall.

Help us in the Church –

When we confuse absence of conflict with the peace of God.
When we equate the shaping of ecclesiastical structures with serving you in
the world.
When we imagine that our task is to preserve rather than to put at risk.
When we behave as though your presence in life were a past event
rather than a contemporary encounter.

Lord, help us when we are tempted:
And save us when we fall.

Help us in the world –
When we use meaningless chatter to avoid real dialogue.
When we allow the image presented by the media to blind us to
the substance that lies behind it.
When we confuse privilege with responsibility and claim rights
when we should be acknowledging duties.
When we allow high sounding reasons to cover evil actions.

Lord, help us when we are tempted:
And save us when we fall.

We pray for our families and our friends and hold them before you in our
thoughts . . .
We especially pray for any who may be under particular pressures and stress
at this time . . .

Lord, help us when we are tempted:
And save us when we fall.

Lord Jesus, you have passed through the test of suffering
and are able to help those who are meeting their test now.
We pray for all who suffer . . .
We especially pray for those who suffer through their own folly or the folly
or malice of others . . .

Lord, help us when we are tempted:
And save us when we fall.

Before the throne of God, where we may find mercy and timely help,
we remember those who have departed this life . . .
Dying, Christ broke the power of sin and death
that we might enter with him into the life eternal.

Lord, help us when we are tempted:
And save us when we fall.
Amen.

Thursday

Lord, we often fold our hands in prayer,
when we should really jump for joy
because you come to us as rescuer, as Savior,
cleaning up the mess we make of our lives,
putting together what we pull apart.

Tell out, my soul, the greatness of the Lord.
Rejoice, my spirit, in God my Savior.

We pray for the Church.
You have called us to have a part in its life
and despite our failures, you have not cast us off.

Tell out, my soul, the greatness of the Lord.
Rejoice, my spirit, in God my Savior.

We know that much of the Church's life and witness
looks silly and weak in the eyes of the world at large,
but you still use its foolishness to shame worldly wisdom
and its weakness to witness against the abuse of power.

Tell out, my soul, the greatness of the Lord.
Rejoice, my spirit, in God my Savior.

We pray for those who cry desperately for salvation
for tyranny to be overthrown
for the despised to be given dignity
for the poor to receive a proper share of the earth's resources.
You are the source of hope and the inspiration to action.

Tell out, my soul, the greatness of the Lord.
Rejoice, my spirit, in God my Savior.

We bring you particular needs . . .
With confidence we share these with you
for you are the God who lives among us.

Tell out, my soul, the greatness of the Lord.
Rejoice, my spirit, in God my Savior.

We pray for our families . . .
Your human life brought both pain and joy to your earthly relatives.
Help us also to know you in both the joys and the pains of family life.

Tell out, my soul, the greatness of the Lord.

Rejoice, my spirit, in God my Savior.

We remember those who have died . . .
Through our sorrow and sense of loss we are glad
for the promise that there shall be an end to death,
and to mourning and crying and pain;
for the old order has passed away.

Tell out, my soul, the greatness of the Lord.
Rejoice, my spirit, in God my Savior.
Amen.

Friday

Lord Jesus, in a dark hour
you spoke of the gift of peace;
we beg that gift for ourselves, that we may have
the inner serenity that cannot be taken from us.
Then we may be messengers of your peace
to a strife-torn world.

Give peace in our time, Lord.
Help us to live in peace.

We pray for those who are fighting,
injury, disfigurement, and death their constant companions,
nerves and bodies strained beyond endurance,
the streams of compassion drying up within them,
their only goal the destruction of the "enemy."
Whatever the color of their skin – we pray for them.
Whatever the sound of their tongue – we pray for them.
Whatever the insignia they wear – we pray for them.

Give peace in our time, Lord.
Help us to live in peace.

We pray for all who have been broken in battle;
for those who weep and those who can no longer weep;
for those who feel the anguish and for those who have lost the capacity to feel;
for all prisoners – and all prison guards;
for those who exist in war-torn lands and for those who no longer have a homeland.

Give peace in our time, Lord.
Help us to live in peace.

We pray for all who stir up strife;
for all who make a profit out of the misery of others;
for all who are led into vice
as they seek a momentary forgetfulness;
for all who believe that war is inevitable.

Give peace in our time, Lord.
Help us to live in peace.

The desire to press self-interest is deeply rooted in us.
We defend our attitudes when we should be ashamed of them.
We compare the noblest aspects of our own cause with the basest of that of
our opponents.
We are reluctant to admit that our own selfish desires could contribute to the
miseries of others.

Give peace in our time, Lord.
Help us to live in peace.

We bring to you particular needs . . .
and we remember those who have died . . .

Give peace in our time, Lord.
Help us to live in peace.
Amen.

Saturday

Spirit of power,
we find it hard to come together in the Church
even within a single congregation.
How shall we learn to be one family
loving and serving the whole of humankind?
Lead us into such unity of purpose
that we may receive power:
not the power to threaten or destroy
but the power to restore waste places.
Use us to declare your glory
that blind eyes may see, deaf ears hear,
and the cynical be brought to faith.

Spirit of the Living God,
Hear our prayer.

Spirit of truth,
we live in a modern Babel

where words are used to conceal meaning
rather than make it plain.
Lead the peoples of the world into such a love of truth
that nation may speak with nation,
not seeking to confuse
but to understand and to be understood,
whereby trust is created, out of which
a truly international community may be born.

Spirit of the Living God,
Hear our prayer.

Creator Spirit,
you give to the old the capacity
to dream dreams and to the young to see visions,
but because we exalt ourselves and our desires
to the place that is yours alone,
our visions are visions of horror
and our dreams nightmares.
Raise up artists and prophets among us
with the will and the ability
to inspire and cleanse our society,
to set our hearts aflame and turn our eyes to the heights.

Spirit of the Living God,
Hear our prayer.

Source of all comfort, we pray for the lonely, the sick, the sad,
the bereaved and all who suffer or are ill at ease . . .
We claim for them the gift of your peace,
that their troubled hearts may be set at rest
and their fears banished.

Spirit of the Living God,
Hear our prayer.

Giver of life, we remember those who have died . . .
May they enter into the Kingdom
where your presence is all in all.

Spirit of the Living God,
Hear our prayer.
Amen.

40

Sunday

Crucified and risen Lord,
we pray for the Church.
Save us from dawdling by an empty tomb.
Save us from bondage to the past.
Save us from the hypnotic fascination of decay and death
and make your Church to know your resurrection life.
May we follow where you lead
and live for you in today's world.

The Lord is risen.
He is risen indeed.

Savior Christ, we pray for the whole human family.
Hanging on the cross
you gave hope to a rebel at your side
and prayed for those who condemned you to that violent death.
We too live amid violence,
the violence of subversion, of repressive government,
and all the subtle violence by which the powerful
seek to impose their will on the weak.
None of us is free from its taint.
You alone can give victory over the violence of the world
and of our hearts.
Save us, Lord.
Give us the will and the power to share your victory.

The Lord is risen.
He is risen indeed.

Living Lord, we pray for our society,
entombed in material possessions
and oppressed with ever-changing fears.
Many know no better hope than that things may get no worse
and that they may enjoy a few years of quiet retirement before the end.
Release us from this living death.
Cause us to live with the life you alone can give.

The Lord is risen.
He is risen indeed.

Lord, you know what it is to suffer pain, degradation, and rejection and to
die an outcast.
We pray for all who suffer . . .
May they know you as one who shares their agony

and enables them to share your triumph.

The Lord is risen.
He is risen indeed.

With thanksgiving for the life that was given
and joyous hope of the life that is yet to be
we remember those who have died . . .
As in Adam all die,
so in Christ will all be brought to life.

The Lord is risen.
He is risen indeed.
Amen.

THE DAILY OFFICE REVISED*

The Christian

•16 The Humanity of Christ

O good Jesus, Word of the Father:
Convert us.

O good Jesus, Son of Mary:
Make us obedient.

O good Jesus, Prince of peace:
Give us peace.

O good Jesus, model of patience:
Help us to persevere.

O good Jesus, meek and humble of heart:
Help us to become like you.

O good Jesus, our Redeemer:
Save us.

O good Jesus, the true Way:
Direct us.

O good Jesus, eternal Truth:
Instruct us.

O good Jesus, Life everlasting:
Make us alive in you.

O good Jesus, our Support:
Strengthen us.

O good Jesus, our Mediator with the Father:
Reconcile us.

O good Jesus, Physician of the soul:
Heal us.

O good Jesus, our Judge:
Absolve us.

O good Jesus, our King:
Govern us.

O good Jesus, our Sanctification:
Sanctify us.

O good Jesus, Living Bread from heaven:
Fill us.

O good Jesus, Father of the prodigal:
Receive us.

O good Jesus, Joy of the soul:
Refresh us.

O good Jesus, our Helper:
Assist us.

O good Jesus, our Protector:
Defend us.

O good Jesus, our Hope:
Sustain us.

O good Jesus, Fountain of life:
Cleanse us.

O good Jesus, our Last End:
Let us come to you.

O good Jesus, our Glory:
Glorify us.
Amen.

KYRIE ELEISON

•17 The Life of Jesus

The Response to each line is: "Have mercy on us."

God the Father, Creator of heaven and earth, *(Response.)*
God the Son, Redeemer of the world,
God the Holy Ghost, Sanctifier of the faithful,

Holy Trinity, one God,
Jesus, sent into the world by the Father,
Jesus, conceived by the Holy Ghost, and born of the Virgin Mary,
Jesus, wrapped in swaddling clothes and laid in a manger,
Jesus, manifesting thyself to the shepherds and adored by the wise men,
Jesus, presented in the temple and submitting to the law of circumcision,
Jesus, persecuted by Herod and exiled into Egypt,
Jesus, brought up at Nazareth and found in the temple in the midst of the
    teachers,
Jesus, baptized by John and tempted in the wilderness,
Jesus, choosing for thy disciples the poor and ignorant and ministering to the
    afflicted,
Jesus, transfigured on the mountain and weeping over Jerusalem,
Jesus, entering Jerusalem as King of Peace and driving the buyers and sellers
    from the temple,
Jesus, washing your disciples' feet and eating the Passover with your
    disciples,
Jesus, giving your Body for food and your Blood for drink,
Jesus, praying in the Garden of Olives and betrayed by Judas,
Jesus, scourged and crowned with thorns and crucified between two thieves,
Jesus, dying upon the Cross and rising again for our justification,
Jesus, ascending into heaven and sitting at the right hand of the Father,
Jesus, sending down on your disciples the Holy Ghost the Comforter,
Jesus, our Judge and our Savior, *Have mercy on us, now and always.*
Amen.

KYRIE ELEISON

•18 For Christ's Strength and Protection

Come quickly, Jesus, the Helper of all:
Come quickly and help us.

You that make broken bodies and lives whole again:
Come quickly and help us.

You that pronounce the blessedness of the poor and of the suffering:
Come quickly and help us.

You that alone bring true freedom to all the nations:
Come quickly and help us.

You that fearlessly denounce the crimes of the powerful:
Come quickly and help us.

You that observe the lilies of the field and the sparrow's fall:
Come quickly and help us.

You that in your coming restore the paradise of Eden:
Come quickly and help us.

You that love children, join the marriage feast, and mourn the dead:
Come quickly and help us.

You that call sinners among the people, and sinners against the people, into
one community:
Come quickly and help us.

You that took on our guilt, so that we could take on your wholeness:
Come quickly and help us.

You that throw the demonic powers out of our lives:
Come quickly and help us.

You that led the march of protest to the Temple of God:
Come quickly and help us.

You that passed through the dark waters, and were anointed with the Spirit:
Come quickly and help us.

You that were lifted up in transfiguration and in brutality:
Come quickly and help us.

You that broke the evil powers by offering yourself to them:
Come quickly and help us.

You that refresh all people with the bread of life and the fruit of the vine:
Come quickly and help us.

Come quickly, our Helper, and pour out your spirit on all your fellow-
servants:
Come quickly and help us.

O Spirit of God's breath, Spirit of our Liberator's life: this community is
dead unless you are the very air it breathes. Come and fulfill the dream of
your saints that a new society will rise out of the ruins of the old. As you
have always in the past come upon those who trusted you, today fill us
who ask only that we may do your work in your strength, to the glory of
God's name.
Amen.

THE COVENANT OF PEACE – A LIBERATION PRAYER BOOK

•19 St. Patrick's Breastplate

Christ be with me,
Christ within me,
Christ behind me,
Christ before me,
Christ beside me, Christ to win me,
Christ to comfort and restore me,

Christ beneath me,
Christ above me,
Christ in quiet,
Christ in danger,
Christ in hearts of all that love me,
Christ in mouth of friend and stranger. Amen.

IRISH, 5TH CENTURY
–TRANSLATED BY CECIL FRANCES ALEXANDER*

•20 Friday Morning

O Jesus, poor and abject, unknown and despised, have mercy upon me;
let me not be ashamed to follow thee.

O Jesus, hated and persecuted, have mercy upon me;
let me not be afraid to come after thee.

O Jesus, betrayed and sold at a vile price, have mercy upon me;
make me content to be as my Master.

O Jesus, blasphemed, accused, and wrongfully condemned, have mercy upon me;
teach me to endure the contradiction of sinners.

O Jesus, clothed with reproach and shame, have mercy upon me;
let me not seek my own glory.

O Jesus, insulted, mocked, and spat upon, have mercy upon me;
let me run with patience the race set before me.

O Jesus, dragged to the pillar, scourged, and bathed in blood, have mercy upon me;
let me not faint in the fiery trial.

O Jesus, crowned with thorns and hailed in derision;
have mercy upon me.

O Jesus, burdened with our sins and the curses of the people;
heve mercy upon me.

O Jesus, affronted, outraged, and buffeted;
have mercy upon me.

O Jesus, overwhelmed with injuries, griefs, and humiliations;
have mercy upon me.

O Jesus, hanging on the accursed Tree, bowing the head, giving up the ghost,
have mercy upon me;
conform my whole soul to thy holy, humble, suffering Spirit.
Amen.

JOHN WESLEY*

•21 For Disciples

Jesus said: "Whoever among you wants to be great must become the servant of all. For the Son of Man himself has not come to be served but to serve, and to give his life to set many others free."
Master, we hear your call;
Lord Jesus, help us to follow.

Jesus said: "Unless you change your whole outlook and become like little children, you will never enter the kingdom of heaven."
Master, we hear your call;
Lord Jesus, help us to follow.

Jesus said: "Blessed are the poor in spirit, for theirs is the kingdom of heaven. Blessed are the meek, for they shall inherit the earth."
Master, we hear your call;
Lord Jesus, help us to follow.

Jesus said: "You must love your enemies, and do good without expecting any return and without giving up hope on anyone: so will you be children of the Most High, because God indeed is kind to the ungrateful and wicked. Be compassionate, as your Father is compassionate."
Master, we hear your call;
Lord Jesus, help us to follow.

Jesus said: "This is my Father's glory, that you may bear fruit in plenty and so be my disciples. If you dwell in me, as I dwell in you, you will bear much fruit; for apart from me you can do nothing."
Master, we hear your call;

Lord Jesus, help us to follow.

Jesus said: "There is no greater love than this, that you should lay down your life for your friends. This is my commandment; love one another, as I have loved you."
Master, we hear your call;
Lord Jesus, help us to follow.

Jesus said: "All power in heaven and on earth has been given to me. You, then, are to go and make disciples of all the nations and baptize them in the name of the Father and of the Son and of the Holy Spirit. Teach them to observe all that I have commanded you. And remember, I am with you always, even to the end of the world."
Master, we hear your call;
Lord Jesus, help us to follow.
Amen.

CONTEMPORARY PRAYERS FOR PUBLIC WORSHIP

• 22 For All Who Have Been Baptized

Let us pray, asking for the grace to remain ever faithful to the new life to which we have been born in water and the Spirit.

(Silence)

Christ Jesus, our rock and salvation, baptism makes us one with you in the kingdom of your Church.
Build your kingdom within us.

Christ Jesus, you offered living water to the Samaritan woman.
Lead us to the fountain of life.

Christ Jesus, you restored life to the widow's son.
Raise us from our death of sin.

Christ Jesus, you gave sight to the man born blind.
Lord, that we may see!

Christ Jesus, you made the lepers clean again.
Lord, if you will, you can make us clean.

Christ Jesus, you are the Good Samaritan who heals our wounds.
Take pity on us, heal the wounds which sin has made on us.

Christ Jesus, Lord and Master of all, you calmed the fury of the storm.
Lord, save us lest we perish.

Christ Jesus, the words of your teaching filled the crowds with astonishment.
You have the words of eternal life.

Christ Jesus, by your word you drove the unclean spirits from the sinful Mary Magdalene.
Protect us from the evil spirit.

Christ Jesus, you gave the crippled man the power to walk again.
Guide our faltering steps in the way of eternal life.

Let us pray, entreating the Lord to strengthen us with his life.

(Silence)

O Lord our God, you came to the rescue of your chosen people in the desert. Fill us, we pray you, with the strength and support of your life so that, always secure in the comfort of your presence, we may labor day by day for the building of your kingdom; through Christ our Lord.
Amen.

SCRIPTURE SERVICES

•23 The Beatitudes

Jesus said: Happy are the poor in spirit; theirs is the kingdom of heaven.

God our Father: help us to know that away from you we have nothing. Save us from pride that mistakes your gifts for possessions; and keep us humble enough to see that we are poor sinners who always need you.

Happy are the poor in spirit.

Thank you, God, for your Son Jesus, who, though he was rich, became poor to live among us; who had no place for himself on earth. By his weakness we are made strong, and by his poverty, rich.

Happy are the poor in spirit;

Theirs is the kingdom of heaven.

Jesus said: Happy are those who mourn; they shall be comforted.

God our Father: we are discouraged by evil and frightened by dying, and have no word of hope within ourselves. Unless you speak to us, O God, we shall be overcome by grieving and despair.

Happy are those who mourn.

Thank you, God, for Jesus Christ, who on the cross faced evil, desertion, and death. You raised him in triumph over every dark power to be our Savior. We give thanks for the hope we have in him.

Happy are those who mourn;

They shall be comforted.

Jesus said: Happy are the gentle; they shall inherit the earth.

God our Father: restrain our arrogance and show us our place on earth. Keep us obedient, for we are your servants, unwise and unworthy, who have no rights and deserve no honors.

Happy are the gentle.

Thank you, God, for Jesus Christ our Master, who did not call us slaves, but your sons and daughters. Help us to work with him, ordering all things for joy, according to your will.

Happy are the gentle;

They shall inherit the earth.

Jesus said: Happy are those who hunger and thirst for what is right; they shall be satisfied.

God our Father: stir up in us a desire for justice, and a love of your law. May we never live carelessly or selfishly, but in all our dealing with neighbors may we look for the right and do it.

Happy are those who hunger and thirst for what is right.

Thank you, God, for Jesus Christ, who overturned rules of human making, yet lived your law in perfect love. Give us freedom to live with your Spirit in justice, mercy, and peace.

Happy are those who hunger and thirst for what is right;

They shall be satisfied.

Jesus said: Happy are the merciful; they shall have mercy shown to them.

God our Father: we do not forgive as you have forgiven us. We nurse old wrongs and let resentments rule us. We tolerate evil in ourselves, yet harshly judge our neighbors. God, forgive us.

Happy are the merciful.

Thank you, God, for your Son Jesus, who gave his life for sinners; who on the cross forgave unforgivable things. Receiving his mercy, may we always forgive.

Happy are the merciful;

They shall have mercy shown to them.

Jesus said: Happy are the pure in heart; they shall see God.

God our Father: we are not pure. We do not live in love. The good we do, we admire too much; we keep score of our virtues. Deliver us, O God, from a divided heart.

Happy are the pure in heart.

Thank you, God, for Jesus Christ, whose words and deeds were pure. By his life our lives are justified, and by his death we are redeemed. In him we see you face to face, and praise you for your goodness.

Happy are the pure in heart;

They shall see God.

Jesus said: Happy are the peacemakers; they shall be called children of God.

God our Father: we have not lived in peace. We have spread discord, prejudice, gossip, and fear among neighbors. Help us, for we cannot help ourselves. Show us your way of peace.

Happy are the peacemakers.

Thank you, God, for Jesus Christ, who has broken down dividing walls of hate to make one family on earth. As he has reconciled us to you, may we be reconciled to one another, living in peace with all your children everywhere.

Happy are the peacemakers;

They shall be called children of God.

Jesus said: Happy are those who are persecuted in the cause of right; theirs is the kingdom of heaven.

God our Father: we are afraid to risk ourselves for the right. We have grown accustomed to wrong and been silent in the face of injustice. Give us anger without hate, and courage to obey you no matter what may happen.

Happy are those who are persecuted in the cause of right.

Thank you, God, for Jesus Christ, who was persecuted for what he said and did; who took the cross upon himself for our sake. May we stand with him in justice and love, and follow where he leads, even to a cross.

Happy are those who are persecuted in the cause of right;

Theirs is the kingdom of heaven.

Jesus said: Happy are you when people abuse you and persecute you and speak all kinds of evil against you on my account. Rejoice and be glad, for your reward will be great in heaven.

God our Father: give us a will to live by your commandments. Keep us from slander, cruelty, and mocking talk, so that we may be faithful witnesses to Jesus Christ our Lord.

Happy are you when people abuse you and persecute you and speak all kinds of evil against you on my account.

We praise you, O God, for your Son Jesus, who called us to be disciples. Give us grace to confess him before the world, and faith to believe he suffered for us. We ask no rewards, only that you make us brave.

Happy are you when people abuse you and persecute you and speak all kinds of evil against you on my account;

Rejoice and be glad, for your reward will be great in heaven.

You are the light of the world. Your light must shine in the sight of all, so that, seeing your good works, they may give praise to your Father in heaven.

Amen.

THE WORSHIPBOOK

• 24 The Mind of Christ

"Let your bearing towards one another arise out of your life in Christ Jesus."

(Philippians 2:5)

Let us then remember Jesus:
Who, though he was rich, yet for our sakes became poor and dwelt among us.
Who was content to be subject to his parents, the child of a poor couple's home.
May this mind be in us that was in Christ Jesus.

Who lived for nearly thirty years an ordinary life, earning his living with his own hands and refusing no humble tasks.

Whom the common people heard gladly, for he understood their ways.

May this mind be in us that was in Christ Jesus.

Let us remember Jesus:

Who was mighty in deed, healing the sick and the disordered, using for others the powers he would not invoke for himself.

Who refused to force anyone's allegiance.

May this mind be in us that was in Christ Jesus.

Who was Master and Lord to his disciples, yet was among them as their companion and as one who served.

Whose meat was to do the will of the Father who sent him.

May this mind be in us that was in Christ Jesus.

Let us remember Jesus:

Who loved people, yet retired from them to pray, rose a great while before day, watched through a night, stayed in the wilderness, went up into a mountain, sought a garden.

Who when he would help a tempted disciple, prayed for him.

May this mind be in us that was in Christ Jesus.

Who prayed for the forgiveness of those who rejected him, and for the perfecting of those who received him.

Who observed good customs, but defied conventions which did not serve the purposes of God.

Who hated sin because he knew the human cost of pride and selfishness, of cruelty and impurity, and still more the cost to his Father in heaven.

May this mind be in us that was in Christ Jesus.

Let us remember Jesus:

Who believed in people to the last and never despaired of them.

Who through all disappointment never lost heart.

Who disregarded his own comfort and convenience, and thought first of others' needs, and though he suffered long, was always kind.

May this mind be in us that was in Christ Jesus.

Who, when he was reviled, reviled not again, and when he suffered, threatened not.

Who humbled himself and carried obedience to the point of death, even death on the cross, and endured faithful to the end.

May this mind be in us that was in Christ Jesus.

O Christ, our only Savior, so come to dwell in us that we may go forth with the light of your hope in our eyes, and with your faith and love in our hearts.

Amen.

THE KINGDOM, THE POWER AND THE GLORY

•25 For a Closer Walk with God

Eternal Father, you have given us knowledge of yourself through the faithful ministry of your Son. Help us by faith to join the ranks of Christ's disciples, and to learn from him at first hand.
Help us so to do, O Lord.

We remember with thankfulness our Lord's love of life, his identity with the ordinary folk, his joy in good companionship, and his delight in the beauty and grandeur of your world.
Increase our joy, O Lord.

We remember how he used his freedom to do your will regardless of the consequences; how he chose the way of sacrificial love rather than the way of personal convenience and moral compromise; and how he used his power by not using it.
Increase our love, O Lord.

We remember how his faithfulness to you led him from Galilee to Jerusalem, and from Jerusalem to the Cross, where he died for us sinners.
Increase our loyalty to you, O Lord.

We remember that you did not desert your Son on the Cross, nor leave him to the triumph of the tomb; but that you raised him in glory and victory on the eighth day of creation, the New Day of the Lord.
Increase our strength, O Lord.

Help us never to be forgetful of the great things you have accomplished through the work of your Son, and to follow him with joy wherever he may lead us.
Increase our faith, O Lord.

Our time is one of despair and expectation, despair because of our inability to save ourselves, of expectation because of our hope that you will raise up for yourself, out of the wilderness of our complacency, a loyal and victorious people.
Increase our hope, O Lord.

Redeem our times, O Father, and guide us in the way of righteousness and truth and peace, of faith and hope and love.
Increase our desire to serve you, O Lord.

You are our God, and we are your people, therefore help us to be faithful to you at all times, and to overcome every evil in the power of the Holy Spirit.
And to your Name be the praise and the glory, for ever, and ever. Amen.

ERNEST GORDON
–PRAYERS AND OTHER RESOURCES FOR PUBLIC WORSHIP

• 26 The Way, the Truth, the Life

He is the Way.
Follow Him through the Land of Unlikeness;
You will see rare beasts, and have unique adventures.

Thou art the Way, to thee alone
From sin and death we flee;
And all who would the Father seek,
Must seek him, Lord, by thee.

He is the Truth.
Seek Him in the Kingdom of Anxiety;
You will come to a great city that has expected your return for years.

Thou art the Truth, thy word alone
True wisdom can impart;
Thou only canst inform the mind
And purify the heart.

He is the Life.
Love Him in the World of the Flesh;
And at your marriage all its occasions shall dance for joy.

Thou art the life, the rending tomb
Proclaims thy conqu'ring arm;
And those who put their trust in thee
Nor death nor hell shall harm.

Thou art the Way, the Truth, the Life:
Grant us that way to know,
That truth to keep, that life to win,
Whose joys eternal flow. Amen.

W. H. AUDEN FROM "FOR THE TIME BEING"
–HYMN STANZAS BY GEORGE WASHINGTON DOANE*

• 27 Christ in All Things

Let us pray, asking for the grace to find God in all things.

(Silence)

Christ our Lord, we find you at the heart of all creation.
We praise you, we worship you, we serve you.

Christ our Lord, we feel your presence in the midst of your Church.

We praise you, we worship you, we serve you.

Christ our Lord, Master of history and of time, you are continually at work in us and in people everywhere.
We praise you, we worship you, we serve you.

Christ our Lord, you do not cease to carry on the work of redemption in our lives.
We praise you, we worship you, we serve you.

Christ our Lord, you have plunged us into your life by our Baptism.
We praise you, we worship you, we serve you.

Christ our Lord, each day you renew and prolong the sacrament of our salvation in the Eucharist.
We praise you, we worship you, we serve you.

Christ our Lord, how many times you have forgiven us our trespasses in the sacrament of penance!
We praise you, we worship you, we serve you.

Christ our Lord, your word in Holy Scripture is full of life and penetrates deeper than any two-edged sword.
We praise you, we worship you, we serve you.

Christ our Lord, you pour out your Spirit of Love to join us more closely with you and the Father.
We praise you, we worship you, we serve you. Amen.

SCRIPTURE SERVICES

• 28 The Spirit of Jesus

Each section may be used separately, or the whole may be used as one continuous litany.

1. In the Ministry of Jesus

Holy Spirit,
who came upon the Virgin Mary
so that she became the mother of Jesus,   (Luke 1:34)
   we pray to you:
Open our hearts to your word,
help us to receive Jesus, the Word of God.

Holy Spirit,
who came upon Zechariah, Elizabeth, and Simeon,   (Luke 1:41, 67)
and helped them recognize the Messiah,   (Luke 2:26)

we pray to you:
Enlighten the eyes of our hearts
so that we may know how to recognize Jesus, the Lord.

Holy Spirit,   (Matthew 3:16)
who came upon Christ Jesus   (Mark 1:10)
when he was baptized in the waters of the Jordan,   (Luke 3:22)
    we pray to you:
Baptize us in the fire of your love
so that the Father may say to each of us: (Matthew 3:17)
"You are my beloved;   (Luke 3:22)
on you my favor rests."

Holy Spirit,   (Matthew 4:1)
who led Christ Jesus   (Mark 1:12)
out into the desert of temptation,   (Luke 4:1)
    we pray to you:
Give us the strength
to conquer in ourselves the power of evil.

Holy Spirit,
who sent Christ Jesus   (Matthew 12:18-21)
to carry the Good News to the poor,   (Luke 4:18-19)
    we pray to you:
Help us to continue your work
by serving the poor, our brothers and sisters.

Holy Spirit,
who spoke the truth by the mouth of despised disciples,   (Matthew 10:20)
    we pray to you:
Place in us your words of wisdom;   (Luke 13:11)
help us to conquer evil by good.   (Romans 12:21)

2. In the Acts of the Apostles

Spirit of Jesus,
poured out in flames of fire upon your disciples   (Acts 2:1-11)
on the day of Pentecost,   (Acts 4:31)
    we pray to you:
Set afire the hearts of your faithful
so that they will announce in all the languages of the world
the wonders of the salvation of God.

Holy Spirit,
who led the deacon Philip on the road from Gaza
to the meeting with the eunuch of the queen of Ethiopia
and had him announce the Good News of Jesus,   (Acts 8:26-40)

we pray to you:
Lead your missionaries
toward all those who are seeking the truth.

Holy Spirit,
who built up the infant churches   (Acts 9:31)
and filled them with your consolation,
    we pray to you:
Make the Kingdom of God on earth
grow by your joy and your peace.

Holy Spirit,
who called Paul and Barnabas
to their mission among the pagans   (Acts 13:4)
and filled them with the joy
of announcing the Good News,   (Acts 13:52)
    we pray to you:
Today bring to life some fervent witnesses for Christ.

Holy Spirit,
who helped the apostles at the council of Jerusalem
and inspired their decisions,   (Acts 15:28)
    we pray to you:
Enlighten those in authority
that their ministry
will be of service to their brothers and sisters. (Acts 20:28)

Holy Spirit,
you who pointed out the way for your disciples
to announce the Gospel,   (Acts 16:6-8)
    we pray to you:
As in the time of the apostles,
guide today's messengers of the Good News.

3. In the Life of the Church

Spirit of Jesus,
you pour the love of God into our hearts;   (Romans 5:5)
    we pray to you:
Enflame all our lives
with the fire of your love.

Holy Spirit,
you raised Christ Jesus from the dead;   (Romans 8:11)
    we pray to you:
Stamp upon us the seal of eternal life.

59

Spirit of Jesus,
you make us holy temples
to the glory of the Father;
   we pray to you:
Help us to glorify God in our bodies.   (I Corinthians 6:19-20)

Holy Spirit,
you distribute your gifts
for the common good of the whole Church;   (I Corinthians 12:4-11)
   we pray to you:
Let the variety of gifts and of ministries
strengthen the unity of the whole body
that all may be loved in the Church
for the special work they accomplish.

Holy Spirit,
in you we have been baptized
to form only one Body;   (I Corinthians 12:13)
   we pray to you:
Gather together all Christians
in the unity of your Church.

Spirit of Jesus,
wherever you reign,   (II Corinthians 3:17)
there freedom triumphs;
   we pray to you:
Lead us to the complete truth,   (John 16:13)
so that your truth will make us free.   (John 8:32)

Spirit of truth,   (John 14:17)
whom the Father sends in the name of the Son,
   we pray to you:
Recall to our memories the words of Jesus   (John 14:26)
and keep them in our hearts.
Amen.

LUCIEN DEISS

•29 The Work of the Spirit

O Lord, who hast set before us the great hope that thy kingdom shall come on earth, and hast taught us to pray for its coming, make us ever ready to thank thee for the signs of its dawning, and to pray and work for that perfect day when thy will shall be done on earth as it is in heaven.

For the work of thy Spirit within and beyond the bounds of thy visible Church,
We thank thee, O Lord.

For the work of thy Spirit in the history of the world, through peaceful advance, and through pain and tumult,
We thank thee, O Lord.

For the work of thy Spirit in the history of our own country, through its heros and leaders, in politics, law, and industry,
We thank thee, O Lord.

For the work of thy Spirit in science and commerce, in literature and art,
We thank thee, O Lord.

For the work of thy Spirit in the slow triumph of truth over error,
We thank thee, O Lord.

For the work of thy Spirit in the growing desire for unity and harmony, between people of every class and nation,
We thank thee, O Lord.

For the work of thy Spirit in the spread of education, and in the development of a fuller life for individuals, with healthier surroundings and better conditions,
We thank thee, O Lord.

For the work of thy Spirit in the deepening sense of human worth and in the growing respect for womanhood and childhood,
We thank thee, O Lord.

For the work of thy Spirit in the Church, which will not cease till it joins all nations and kindreds and tongues and peoples into one great family, to thy praise and glory,
We thank thee, O Lord. Amen.

THE KINGDOM, THE POWER AND THE GLORY

•30 The Fruit of the Spirit

Let us ask God to give us the fruits of his Spirit in our lives.

Love, that we may love you as you have loved us, and that we may love our neighbors in the world as you love them;
The fruit of the Spirit is love.
Grant us this gift, good Lord.

Joy, that we may be happy ourselves, and that we may help others to be happy;
The fruit of the Spirit is joy.
Grant us this gift, good Lord.

Peace, that we may never again be restless, and worried, and nervous;
The fruit of the Spirit is peace.
Grant us this gift, good Lord.

Patience, that we may no longer be irritable and hurried;
The fruit of the Spirit is patience.
Grant us this gift, good Lord.

Kindness, that we may desire to give rather than to get, to share rather than to keep, to praise rather than to criticize, to forgive rather than to condemn;
The fruit of the Spirit is kindness.
Grant us this gift, good Lord.

Goodness, that we may be an example and a help to all;
The fruit of the Spirit is goodness.
Grant us this gift, good Lord.

Faithfulness, that through all the chances and the changes of life we may be true to ourselves, true to our loved ones, and true to you;
The fruit of the Spirit is faithfulness.
Grant us this gift, good Lord.

Gentleness, that we may be humble and not proud, and that we may never deliberately or carelessly hurt others;
The fruit of the Spirit is gentleness.
Grant us this gift, good Lord.

Self-control, that no moment of impulse or of passion may cause us to injure another or to bring shame on ourselves;
The fruit of the Spirit is self-control
Grant us this gift, good Lord.

Help us so to live
that our lives may reflect
the Spirit of our Lord Jesus Christ,
whose we are
and whom we seek to serve. Amen.

WILLIAM BARCLAY
–EPILOGUES AND PRAYERS

• 31 Calling Upon the Spirit

The Spirit joins with our spirit, alleluia!
To declare that we are children of God, alleluia!

Holy Spirit, Creator! In the beginning you moved over the waters, and from your breath all creatures first drew their life.
Holy Spirit, come!

Holy Spirit, Counsellor! By your inspiration the people of God and the prophets spoke and acted in faith. You clothed them in your power, to be the bearers of your Word.
Holy Spirit, come!

Holy Spirit, Life-giver! You overshadowed the Virgin Mary to make her the mother of the Son of God.
Holy Spirit, come!

Holy Spirit, Sanctifier! By you, Jesus grew in wisdom and grace. On the day of his baptism, you descended on him as a dove to consecrate him and fill him with power to bear witness to the Father.
Holy Spirit, come!

Holy Spirit, Empowerer! By you, the disciples left all at Jesus' call and followed him, proclaiming the glories of his Name to the ends of the earth.
Holy Spirit, come!

Father, in your infinite goodness, set us aflame with that fire of the Spirit Christ brought upon the earth and longed to see ablaze, for he lives and reigns with you and the Spirit now and for ever. *Amen.*

PRAISE GOD: COMMON PRAYER AT TAIZÉ

• 32 A Personal Litany

That it may please thee to grant me by thy Holy Spirit to hear ever more clearly thy voice, calling me to a deeper devotion to thy service:
Lord, hear my prayer.

For grace to respond with my whole heart to thy call:
Lord, hear my prayer.

For a continual sense of thine abiding presence and overruling guidance in my daily life:
Lord, hear my prayer.

For a deeper love and earnestness in the act of consecration to thee of myself, my soul and body, that I make anew at each Communion:
Lord, hear my prayer.

For the illuminating grace of thy Holy Spirit, that I may be guided to use for thee every power and every opportunity thou hast given me:
Lord, hear my prayer.

For grace so to live in the light of thy divine love for me that, loving thee above all, I may give to others the sunshine of love which has its source in thee alone:
Lord, hear my prayer.

For spiritual insight to realize more fully my influence on others, and grace to use it only and always for thee:
Lord, hear my prayer.

For wisdom, taught of love, to understand the needs of my friends, and grace to help them by prayer and sympathy:
Lord, hear my prayer.

For a daily renewal of the spirit of true joy which the sense of thine abiding presence alone can give, that all the joys of my life may be sanctified in thee:
Lord, hear my prayer.

For a steadfast heart to meet with constant cheerfulness the anxieties and trials of my life as thy way of sanctification for me:
Lord, hear my prayer.

For inspiration and grace so to worship thee and to serve thee here, that I may be ready for thy perfect service hereafter:
Lord, hear my prayer.

For a right judgment in giving to each duty its due place and proportion, that my days may be ordered in accordance with thy divine will:
Lord, hear my prayer.

For grace to make the spirit in which I fulfill all social duties one with the spirit of my inmost life and prayers:
Lord, hear my prayer.

For grace to refrain from the unkind word, and from the unkind silence:
Lord, hear my prayer.

For guidance so to use the intellectual ability thou hast given that I may continually go forward towards the fullness of that perfection which thou hast purposed for me:
Lord, hear my prayer.

For a spirit of willing self-denial, that I may give gladly and freely for the work of thy Church at home and abroad:
Lord, hear my prayer.

For inward light to see how far short I have come of thy divine purpose for me:
Lord, hear my prayer.

For a truer penitence, a firmer faith, a deeper devotion, a more perfect love:
Lord, hear my prayer.

For a fuller apprehension of thine infinite love for me – of the power of prayer – of the joy of spiritual things – of the glory that shall be revealed:
Lord, hear my prayer.

And grant unto me, unworthy though I am, a clear vision of the beauty of holiness and a sure confidence that in thy light and by thy grace I may at last attain to it; through thy Son, Jesus Christ. *Amen.*

W. B. TREVELYAN
–PRAYERS FOR A NEW WORLD

• 33 God Be in My Head

God be in My head,
And in my understanding;

God be in mine eyes,
And in my looking;

God be in my mouth,
And in my speaking;

God be in my heart,
And in my thinking;

God be at mine end,
And at my departing. Amen.

SARUM PRIMER 1558*

The Whole Armor of God

• 34 For Grace in All Its Aspects

The grace of a thankful and uncomplaining heart:
Grant this, good Lord.

The grace to wait on your word patiently and to answer your call promptly:
Grant this, good Lord.

The grace of courage, whether in suffering or in danger:
Grant this, good Lord.

The grace to endure privation and discomfort as a good soldier of Jesus Christ:
Grant this, good Lord.

The grace of boldness in standing for what is right:
Grant this, good Lord.

The grace of preparedness, lest I enter into temptation:
Grant this, good Lord.

The grace of bodily discipline:
Grant this, good Lord.

The grace of strict truthfulness:
Grant this, good Lord.

The grace to treat others as I would have others treat me:
Grant this, good Lord.

The grace of charity, that I may refrain from hasty judgement:
Grant this, good Lord.

The grace of silence, that I may refrain from hasty speech:

Grant this, good Lord.

The grace of forgiveness towards all who have wronged me:
Grant this, good Lord.

The grace of tenderness towards all who are weaker than myself:
Grant this, good Lord.

The grace of steadfastness in continuing to desire that you will grant what I now pray for:
Grant this, good Lord. Amen.

JOHN BAILLIE

•35 At the Start of the Day

O God of the ages, grant that we, who are the heirs of all the ages, may not fail to profit by the heavenly wisdom which in time past you have given to your servants.

A wise man wrote,
   The world is too much with us; late and soon,
   Getting and spending, we lay waste our powers.
   O God, give us grace to profit by this word.

A wise man wrote,
   Our wills are ours to make them your own.
   O God, give us grace to profit by this word.

A wise king said,
   Nothing for me is too early or too late which is in due time for you.
   O God, give us grace to profit by this word.

A wise man said,
   Expect great things from God, attempt great things for God.
   O God, give us grace to profit by this word.

A wise man said,
   In his will is our peace.
   O God, give us grace to profit by this word.

A wise woman said,
   The divine moment is the present moment.
   O God, give us grace to profit by this word.

A wise woman said,
   Those to whom God is not sufficient are asking too much.

O God, give us grace to profit by this word.

A wise man prayed,
  Give what you command, and command what you will.
  O God, give us grace to profit by this word.

A wise man prayed,
  My past life hide; my future guide.
  O God, give us grace to profit by this word.

Grant, O Father,
that we may go about this day's business
with an ever-present remembrance
of the great traditions wherein we stand
and the great cloud of witnesses
which at all times surround us,
that thereby we may be kept from evil ways
and inspired to high endeavor.
So keep us until evening
in the might of Jesus Christ our Lord. Amen.

JOHN BAILLIE

• 36 For Obedience to the Will of God

Let us pray, asking the Lord our God to make us always "doers of the word, and not hearers only," deceiving ourselves.

(Silence)

Not everyone who says to me "Lord, Lord," shall enter the kingdom of
  heaven,
but only those who do the will of my Father who is in heaven.
Teach me to do your will,
for you are my God.

And everyone who hears these words of mine and does not act on them,
shall be likened to a foolish man who built his house of sand.
Teach me to do your will,
for you are my God.

"This people honors me with their lips,
but their heart is far from me,"
Teach me to do your will,
for you are my God.

Oh, that today you would hear his voice:
"Harden not your hearts as at Meribah,
as on the day of Massah in the desert."
Teach me to do your will,
for you are my God.

For it is not those who hear the Law that are just in the sight of God;
but it is those who follow the Law who will be justified.
Teach me to do your will,
for you are my God.

For all who do the will of my Father in heaven, they are my brothers and
sisters and mother.
Teach me to do your will,
for you are my God.

"To do your will, O my God, is my delight,
and your law is within my heart!"
Teach me to do your will,
for you are my God.

"My food is to do the will of the One who sent me,
to accomplish that work."
Teach me to do your will,
for you are my God.

My dear children, let us not love in word or in speech,
but in deed and in truth.
Teach me to do your will,
for you are my God for ever and ever. Amen.

SCRIPTURE SERVICES

•37 The Greatest of These Is Love
–I Corinthians 13

Love is patient and kind.

> *O God, help us to be patient with people,*
> *even when they are foolish and annoying;*
> *and help us to be as kind to others*
> *as we would wish them to be to us.*

Love is not jealous or boastful.

> *O God, help us never to grudge other people*

their possessions or successes,
and keep us from all pride and conceit,
that we may never boast of what we are,
or have, or have achieved.

Love is not arrogant or rude.

O God, make us at all times courteous,
and no matter who the other person is,
help us never to look on anyone with contempt.

Love does not insist on its own way; it is not irritable or resentful.

O God, help us not to be irritable
and difficult to live with,
nor to resent criticism or rebuke,
even when we do not deserve it.

Love does not rejoice at wrong, but rejoices in the right.

O God, help us never to find pleasure in any wrong thing,
but to find happiness only in doing the right,
and in helping others to do it.

Love bears all things.

O God, help us to bear insults and slights,
and never to grow bitter.

Love believes all things.

O God, help us never to lose faith
in Jesus our Lord.

Love hopes all things.

O God, help us never to despair,
however dark and difficult and discouraging life may be.

Love endures all things.

O God, help us to stick it out to the end,
and never to give in.

Love never ends. For faith, hope, and love abide, these three; but the greatest of these is love.

O God, you are love;
help us to show your love to others each day of our lives.
This we ask for your love's sake. Amen.

WILLIAM BARCLAY
–EPILOGUES AND PRAYERS

• 38 For Wisdom to Know and Courage to Act

God of grace and God of glory,
On thy people pour thy power;
Crown thine ancient church's story;
Bring its bud to glorious flower.
Grant us wisdom,
Grant us courage,
For the facing of this hour.

Lo! the hosts of evil round us
Scorn thy Christ, assail his ways!
From the fears that long have bound us,
Free our hearts to faith and praise.
Grant us wisdom,
Grant us courage,
For the living of these days.

Cure thy children's warring madness;
Bend our pride to thy control;
Shame our wanton, selfish gladness,
Rich in things and poor in soul.
Grant us wisdom,
Grant us courage,
Lest we miss thy kingdom's goal.

Set our feet on lofty places;
Gird our lives that they may be
Armored with all Christ-like graces
In the fight to set all free.
Grant us wisdom,
Grant us courage,
Lest we fail thy world or thee.

Save us from weak resignation
To the evils we deplore;
Let the search for thy salvation
Be our glory evermore.
Grant us wisdom,
Grant us courage,
Serving thee whom we adore. Amen.

HARRY EMERSON FOSDICK*

•39 Hope in Action

Hope looks for the good in people
instead of harping on the worst.

Hope opens doors
where despair closes them.

Hope discovers what can be done
instead of grumbling about what cannot.

Hope draws its power from a deep trust in God
and the basic goodness of humanity.

Hope "lights a candle"
instead of "cursing the darkness."

Hope regards problems, small or large,
as opportunities to be grasped and used.

Hope cherishes no illusions,
nor does it yield to cynicism.

Hope sets large goals
and is not frustrated by repeated difficulties or setbacks.

Hope pushes ahead
when it would be easy to quit.

Hope puts up with modest gains
realizing that "the longest journey starts with one step."

Hope accepts misunderstanding
as the price for serving the greater good of others.

Hope is a good loser
because it has the divine assurance of final victory.

"In the world you will have trouble, but be brave. I have conquered the
world."   (John 16:33)

*"Thanks be to God, who gives us the victory through our Lord Jesus
Christ."*   (I Corinthians 15:57)
Amen.

JAMES KELLER
–MODELS FOR MINISTERS I*

•40 For Gratitude in Times of Doubt

Blessed Trinity, One God,
Teach us gratitude.

At times when we are filled with doubt,
Doubt you, or miracles, or truth,
And our soul's needs are heavy, arid, tired,
Blessed Trinity, One God,
Teach us gratitude.

If no prayer fits our lips, no praise
Fills our hearts, no song lifts our minds,
And all our searching for you finds us lost,
Blessed Trinity, One God,
Teach us gratitude.

Though our ambitions lie in ashes,
Our efforts vanished in disappointment,
Our identity gone in all we tried to do,
Blessed Trinity, One God,
Teach us gratitude.

Because in such times as these,
We shall learn that
"Faith is the substance of things hoped for,
The evidence of things not seen,"
Blessed Trinity, One God,
Teach us gratitude. Amen.

KAY SMALLZRIED

•41 That We May Live Life Well

Lord God, you have given us life. Help us to live in such a way that we make the contribution to life which you have fitted and equipped us to make.

(Silence)

Help us to remember all that has been done for us and all that we have received.
Lord God, Giver of life,
Keep us from living ungratefully.

Help us to remember that we shall one day answer to you for the way in which we have used everything which you have given us.
Lord God, Giver of life,
Keep us from living irresponsibly.

Grant that we may never bring shame to ourselves or hurt and sorrow to others because we did not stop to think.
Lord God, Giver of life,
Keep us from living carelessly.

Grant that our comfort, our pleasure, our wishes, our aims, our ambitions may not be the only things which matter to us. Help us to remember that we have received our time, our talents, and our money to use, not for ourselves alone, but for our neighbors also.
Lord God, Giver of life,
Keep us from living selfishly.

Grant that we may never foolishly flirt with temptation or play with fire. Help us to have nothing to do with the things which we know are wrong.
Lord God, Giver of life,
Keep us from living dangerously.

Help us to take our full part in the life and work and service of the community.
Lord God, Giver of life,
Keep us from living unsocially.

Grant that we may never shut any person out of our church or our community because of color, party, sex or creed.
Lord God, Giver of life,
Keep us from living exclusively. Amen.

WILLIAM BARCLAY
–EPILOGUES AND PRAYERS

•42 Hearing and Heeding

Jesus Christ said, Do not lay up for yourselves treasures on earth, but lay up for yourselves treasures in heaven.
O God, incline our hearts to follow in this way.

Jesus Christ said, Seek first the kingdom of God and his righteousness.
O God, incline our hearts to follow in this way.

Jesus Christ said, Do good and lend, hoping for nothing in return.
O God, incline our hearts to follow in this way.

Jesus Christ said, Love your enemies.
O God, incline our hearts to follow in this way.

Jesus Christ said, Watch and pray, that you do not enter into temptation.
O God, incline our hearts to follow in this way.

Jesus Christ said, Fear not, only believe.
O God, incline our hearts to follow in this way.

Jesus Christ said, Except you turn again and become as little children, you shall not enter into the kingdom of heaven.
O God, incline our hearts to follow in this way.

Jesus Christ said, Ask and it shall be given you; seek, and you shall find; knock, and it shall be opened to you.
O God, incline our hearts to follow in this way. Amen.

JOHN BAILLIE

•43 For Spiritual Growth

As our knowledge grows larger,
increase our love of the truth.

As our arms grow stronger,
increase our respect for love.

As our world grows smaller,
increase our sense of community.

As our nation grows more divided,
increase our efforts for unity.

As our neighborhood grows more impersonal,
increase our attempts to know each other.

As our families grow up,
increase our interests in others.

As our freedoms grow greater,
increase our powers of self-control.

As our material comforts grow in number,
increase our interest in things of the spirit.

As our institutions grow more complex,
increase our concern for the individual.

As our laws grow more complicated,
increase our hopes for justice.

As our future grows more uncertain,
increase our appreciation for the present.

As our bodies grow older,
increase our faith in the one eternal God. Amen.

LARRY HARD

•44 A Revitalized Ministry

If our lives have become shallow,
deepen them.

If our principles have become shabby,
repair them.

If our ideals have become tarnished,
restore them.

If our hopes have become faded,
revive them.

If our loyalties have grown dim,
brighten them.

If our values have become confused,
clarify them.

If our purposes have become blurred,
sharpen them.

If our horizons have begun to contract,
widen them.

Where there is hatred,
let us bring love.

Where there is wrong,
let us bring pardon.

Where there is error,
let us bring truth.

Where there is doubt,
let us bring faith.

Where there is pain,
let us bring healing.

Where there is darkness,
let us bring light.

Where there is despair,
let us bring hope.

Where there is discord,
let us bring peace.

Where there is sadness,
let us bring joy.

Lord, grant that we may seek rather to comfort than to be comforted;
To understand than to be understood;
To love than to be loved;

For
It is in giving that we receive;
It is in forgiving that we are forgiven;
It is in dying that we awaken to eternal life. Amen.

MODELS FOR MINISTERS I*

•45 Body and Soul

O God, our Father, you have shown us in the works and words of Jesus, your Son, that you care both for our bodies and our souls. Protect us alike in body and soul.
We pray for your blessing on our bodies.
Health for our day's work;
Wisdom to seek the doctor's skill, if we know, or
even suspect, that anything is wrong;
Wisdom neither to overdrive our bodies until we ex-
haust them, nor to allow them to grow weak and
flabby through too much ease;
Wise discipline in our habits, that we may allow
ourselves no indulgences nor become the victim
of any habits which would injure our health:
Grant this, O God.

And since we know that mind and body are linked in-
separably together, grant us a sound mind:
A mind at rest and at peace;

A mind undistressed by worry, and free from anxiety;
A mind cleansed and purified from every evil, every
   bitter and every resentful thought;
A mind determined to do all it can, and then content
   to leave the rest to you:
Grant this, O God.

We pray for your blessing on our souls.
From being so immersed in the world that we forget
   that we have a soul;
From being so busy with the things which are seen
   and temporal that we entirely forget the things
   which are unseen and eternal;
From forgetting that it does not profit us if we gain
   the whole world if in so doing we lose our soul:
Save us, O God.

From the temptations which attack our soul from in-
   side and from outside;
From all habits and practices and ways of life which
   make our soul less sensitive to you;
From all that makes our soul less fit to enter your
   presence when this life ends:
Defend us, O God.

Bless us in body, soul and spirit that we may live this life well, and at the
end of it enter into life eternal; through Jesus Christ our Lord. *Amen.*

WILLIAM BARCLAY
–PRAYERS FOR THE CHRISTIAN YEAR

•46 God Is Our Help and Strength

Eternal God, be our Help;
Eternal God, sustain us;
Eternal God, be our Answer
when we call upon you.

God of all being, be our Help;
Searcher of hearts, sustain us;
Mighty Redeemer, be our Answer
when we call upon you.

Proclaimer of justice, be our Help;

God surrounded by glory, sustain us;
Steadfast and loving One, be our Answer
when we call upon you.

Pure and upright One, be our Help;
Friend of the poor, sustain us;
Inspiration to goodness, be our Answer
when we call upon you.

Mind of the universe, be our Help;
God of power and splendor, sustain us;
Lord arrayed in justice, be our Answer
when we call upon you.

Eternal Ruler, be our Help;
Radiant and glorious God, sustain us;
Upholder of the falling, be our Answer
when we call upon you.

Helper of the weak, be our Help;
Redeemer and Deliverer, sustain us;
Eternal Rock, be our Answer
when we call upon you.

Holy and awesome One, be our Help;
Merciful and gracious God, sustain us;
Keeper of the Covenant, be our Answer
when we call upon you.

Support of the innocent, be our Help;
Mighty for ever, sustain us;
Pure in your ways, be our Answer
when we call upon you. Amen.

GATES OF PRAYER
THE NEW UNION PRAYER BOOK

•47 A Prayer for Help

Most holy and most merciful God, the strength of the weak, the rest of the weary, the comfort of the sorrowful, the savior of the sinful, and the refuge of thy children in every time of need, hear us as we pray for thy help.
Heavenly Father, help us.

When our faith is growing weak, and our love is growing cold, and we are losing the vision of thy face, and the spiritual world is no longer real to us,

Heavenly Father, help us.

When the evil memories of the past trouble us, and we mourn over early dreams and hopes unrealized, over light within us turned to darkness, and strength to weakness,
Heavenly Father, help us.

When we are tempted to mean and wicked ways, and sin grows less sinful in our sight; when duty is difficult and work is hard, and our burdens are heavy,
Heavenly Father, help us.

When the unknown future troubles us, and in our fears and anxieties we forget thy eternal love and mercy; and when the last darkness shall close around us, and heart and flesh fail, and vain is all earthly help,
Heavenly Father, help us.

O God, who knowest us to be set in the midst of so many and great dangers, that by reason of the frailty of our nature we cannot always stand upright, grant to us such strength and protection as may support us in all dangers and carry us through all trials.
Heavenly Father, help us. Amen.

WITH ONE VOICE

•48 For God's Presence at All Times

Let us pray, asking the Lord to make his presence known to us.

(Silence)

When we lose sight of the power you hold as Lord and Master of history –
Stay with us then, O Lord.

When we fail to recognize your presence in the events of our daily life –
Stay with us then, O Lord.

When we do not remember that it is necessary for us to suffer and die with you so as to share your glory –
Stay with us then, O Lord.

When we make our minds dull and foolish so that we do not understand the word that you speak to us –
Stay with us then, O Lord.

When we are tempted to think of your Church as a mere set of restrictions and obligations which weigh upon us –

Stay with us then, O Lord.

When we are inclined not to face the real situations that arise in our lives, but prefer to turn from them and from seeking your holy will in them –
Stay with us then, O Lord.

When our feelings tell us that the trials you send us are a sign that you have abandoned us –
Stay with us then, O Lord.

When our emotions deceive us into thinking that evils are not evil because you permit them,
Stay with us then, O Lord.

When our need for material security makes us confuse good providence with greed –
Stay with us then, O Lord.

When our impulse to show our love for others degenerates into selfish attempts to satisfy our own passions –
Stay with us then, O Lord.

When the representatives of your holy authority are seen by us as merely human, and not as the bearers of your will for us –
Stay with us then, O Lord.

When the day of our life on earth draws towards evening and the hand of death tightens its grip upon us –
Stay with us Lord, then and forever. Amen.

SCRIPTURE SERVICES

•49 A Litany of the Tongue

O God, you have given power to our tongues to create light or darkness in the lives of our friends; help us to keep watch over our words.

Let the words of my mouth, and the meditation of my heart, be acceptable in your sight, O Lord, my Strength and my Redeemer.

From backbiting and talebearing, from uncharitable judgement, from flattery and scandal, from delibrate lie and subtle insincerity, guard our wayward tongues.

Let the words of my mouth, and the meditation of my heart, be acceptable in your sight, O Lord, my Strength and my Redeemer.

We humbly confess before you the harm done by our hasty speech. We have discouraged those we might have helped, embittered those we might have sweetened, exasperated those we might have pacified, depressed those we might have gladdened, misguided those we might have led. Convert, we entreat you, our disordered and ill-tempered tongues.

Create in me a clean heart, O God, and renew a right spirit within me.

Let all bitterness and anger and evil-speaking be put away from us, together with all malice.

Create in me a clean heart, O God, and renew a right spirit within me.

Use our tongues for noble ends. To hearten the dismayed, illumine the benighted, strengthen the weak, comfort the sad; to bring light out of darkness, friendship out of enmity, and joy out of pain.

Guide our lips, O Lord.

May good causes, hard beset by many enemies, be strengthened by our forthright speech. Let not unpopularity affright us nor cowardice detain us from the stout utterance of our best convictions. May no right be denied to anyone, no hopeful movement of your purpose fail for want of our supporting word.

Guide our lips, O Lord.

Forasmuch as we must speak to our own hearts before we can speak to others, watch the inner conversation of our souls. Let not the rudder of our tongues turn the ship of our own spirits into perverse courses. Free our self-communion from every crooked way; let our inner meditation enlighten our outward speech, and may we so wisely talk to ourselves that we can persuasively talk to others.

Have mercy on us, O Lord, and grant us these blessings. Amen.

HARRY EMERSON FOSDICK

• 50 Self-Forgiveness

Lord,
When we are cowards
Who cannot share the travail of your Cross,
You ask God
To forgive us.
Lord, teach us to forgive ourselves.

Lord,
When we are idlers
Who gamble away life's dear resource of time,
You ask God
To forgive us.
Lord, teach us to forgive ourselves.

Lord,
When we are bigots
Who cherish false opinion as the truth,
You ask God
To forgive us.
Lord, teach us to forgive ourselves.

Lord,
When we are grumblers
Who magnify resentments into wrongs,
You ask God
To forgive us.
Lord, teach us to forgive ourselves.

Lord,
When we are hedonists
Who cheat our pleasures of their innocence,
You ask God
To forgive us.
Lord, teach us to forgive ourselves.

Lord,
When we are cynics
Who ambush faith, and war upon God's grace,
You ask God
To forgive us.
Lord, teach us to forgive ourselves.

Lord,
When we are fools
Who must be suffered gladly,
You ask God
To forgive us.
Lord, teach us to forgive ourselves.

Unless, Lord,
We forgive ourselves,
God's great forgiveness
Becomes an affront
So unendurable we seek all means

Whereby we may escape its claim.
But if once we may reach
Behind our masks, and
Replace our subterfuge
With loving courage,
The promise of God's grace awaits us.
Lord, teach us to forgive ourselves. Amen.

KAY SMALLZRIED

†††Prayer and †††Daily Life

Families, Friends
and Neighbors

•51 A Shout of Praise, a Cry of Hope

Leader: Let us not falter in hope! Let us offer our praise and our lives to the Lord.

Men: God of the patriarchs,

Women: God of the matriarchs,

All: *In line with all your faithful people in every age, we offer ourselves and our gifts for the service of your kingdom!*

Women: God of Abraham, Isaac, and Jacob,

Men: God of Sarah, Rebekah, and Rachel,

All: *Grant us the courage to cling to your promise, even if all the world seems hostile and our own hearts judge us failures.*

Men: God of Priscilla and Aquila,

Women: God of Moses and of Miriam,

All: *May we, too, labor in harmony to bring our people out of bondage and darkness.*

Women: O God of Deborah, a mother in Israel,
greatest of Israel's judges,

Men: O God of Solomon, the wisest of kings,

All:	*May our lives be but mirrors of your justice, lived out in the wisdom of unswerving faith.*
Men:	Great God of Lydia, seller of purple,
Women:	Master of Paul, maker of tents,
All:	*Guide us into the world, unafraid to lend our hands, as well as our voices, to your service, and eager to involve ourselves with all of your children.*
Women:	And for the lives of all righteous women,
Men:	And for past and present men of faith,
All:	*For the ministries taking form within us, and for all the callings yet to be: The Lord's name be praised! Amen.*

GAIL ANDERSON RICCIATI
–LITURGY MAGAZINE, MAY 1970*

•52 Men and Women

A woman:	God, whose likeness and image we are,
A man:	you have made us male and female,
A woman:	ordained that our very life come from the union of the sexes,
A man:	fashioned our world in such a way that this distinction is within its very structure.
All:	*For what we are, we give you thanks.*
A woman:	For tenderness and gentleness and pity, for the love of beauty and order and tranquility, and for the instinct to give shelter and nourish and enfold,
All:	*For all that is of woman, we give you thanks.*

A man: For decisiveness and action and strength,
           for the love of precision
           and accomplishment and endeavor,
           for the instinct to protect
           and lead and determine,

All: *For all that is of man,*
           we give you thanks.

A woman: And yet, Lord,
           women can also be strong.
           Why must we be treated as if we were weak
           and incompetent and unworthy?

A man: And, Lord,
           men can also love beauty.
           Why must we be treated as if we were weak
           insensitive and unfeeling?

All: *Help us, Lord, to see ourselves as complete persons,*
           and give us the sense to allow others
           to be themselves.

A woman: Set women free
           from the expectations of others
           and the chains of tradition
           and the pressures of society.

A man: Set men free
           from their need to dominate
           and their fear of change
           and their pride.

All: *Help us, Lord, to be completely human*
           by allowing us to be sexually complete.

A woman: Let women continue to cherish
           homes and families,
           recipes and fashions.

A man: Let men continue to work with
           their hands and minds,
           concerned for athletics
           and tools and motors.

All: *So may it be, Father,*
that as we are, we praise you
by coming together in the order of your creation,
each adding our sexuality
and our being as humans
created by you for your world.

A woman: Increase our respect and regard
one for another,

A man: and teach us to gain from each other
that our lives may be fulfilled,

All: *For we pray in the name of Jesus.*
Amen.

CARL T. UEHLING

•53 For a Couple on Their Wedding Day

Eternal God, creator and preserver of all life, author of salvation, and giver of all grace: Look with favor upon the world you have made, and for which your Son gave his life, and especially upon this man and this woman whom you make one flesh in Holy Matrimony.
Lord, in your mercy,
Hear our prayer.

Give them wisdom and devotion in the ordering of their common life, that each may be to the other a strength in need, a counselor in perplexity, a comfort in sorrow, and a companion in joy.
Lord, in your mercy,
Hear our prayer.

Grant that their wills may be so knit together in your will, and their spirits in your Spirit, that they may grow in love and peace with you and one another all the days of their life.
Lord, in your mercy,
Hear our prayer.

Give them grace, when they hurt each other, to recognize and acknowledge their fault, and to seek each other's forgiveness and yours.
Lord, in your mercy,
Hear our prayer.

Make their life together a sign of Christ's love to this sinful and broken world, that unity may overcome estrangement, forgiveness heal guilt, and joy conquer despair.
Lord, in your mercy,
Hear our prayer.

Bestow on them, if it is your will, the gift and heritage of children, and the grace to bring them up to know you, to love you, and to serve you.
Lord, in your mercy,
Hear our prayer.

Give them such fulfillment of their mutual affection that they may reach out in love and concern for others.
Lord, in your mercy,
Hear our prayer.

Grant that all married persons who have witnessed these vows may find their lives strengthened and their loyalties confirmed.
Lord, in your mercy,
Hear our prayer.

Grant that the bonds of our common humanity, by which all your children are united one to another, and the living to the dead, may be so transformed by your grace, that your will may be done on earth as it is in heaven; where, O Father, with your Son and the Holy Spirit, you live and reign in perfect unity, now and for ever. *Amen.*

THE BOOK OF COMMON PRAYER 1979

•54 In Praise of Marriage

Thanksgiving for Marriage
(Everyone stands and a husband and wife lead an Act of Thanksgiving for Marriage. The people make their reply loudly and with enthusiasm.)

Husband: Let us thank God for our wedding day.

All: *Thanks be to God.*

Wife: Let us thank God for the wonder of falling in love and making love.

All: *Thanks be to God.*

Husband: Let us thank God for our wives.

Husbands: *Thanks be to God.*

Wife:	Let us thank God for our husbands.
Wifes:	*Thanks be to God.*
Husband:	Let us thank God for our homes.
All:	*Thanks be to God.*
Wife:	Let us thank God for our children.
All:	*Thanks be to God.*
Husband:	Let us thank God for our friends.
All:	*Thanks be to God.*
Wife:	Let us thank God for everything.
All:	*Thanks be to God.*

Reaffirmation of Marriage Vows
(The people are seated.)

Husband:	Listen to what St. Paul has to say about marriage, and how he sees in it a mirror of Christ's love for his Church.
Wife:	"Husbands, love your wives, as Christ also loved the Church and gave himself up for it, to consecrate it, cleansing it by water and word, so that he might present the Church to himself all glorious, with no stain or wrinkle or anything of the sort, but holy and without blemish."
Husband:	"In the same way, men also are bound to love their wives, as they love their own bodies. In loving his wife a man loves himself. For no one ever hated his own body; on the contrary he provides and cares for it; and that is how Christ treats the Church, because it is his Body, of which we are living parts."
Wife:	Thus it is that (in the words of Scripture): "A man shall leave his father anad mother and shall be joined to his wife, and the two shall become a single body". It is a great truth that is hidden here.
Husband:	"I for my part refer it to Christ and to the Church, but it applies also individually: each of you must love his wife as his very self;"
Wife:	"And the woman must see to it that she pays her husband all respect."
	(Everyone stands for the Reaffirmation of the Marriage Vows.)

Husband:	I call upon the husbands here to reaffirm their marriage vows, saying with me:
Husbands:	*I reaffirm my solemn promise to my wife to have and to hold, for better, for worse; for richer, for poorer; in sickness and in health; to love and to cherish, till death us do part.*
Wife:	I call upon the wives here to reaffirm their marriage vows to their husbands.
Wives:	*I reaffirm my solemn promise to my husband to have and to hold, for better, for worse; for richer, for poorer; in sickness and in health; to love and to cherish, till death us do part.*

Blessing of Married Couples

Minister: May God the Father, who at creation ordained that man and woman become one flesh, keep you one. *Amen.*

May God the Son, who adorned this manner of life by his first miracle, at the wedding in Cana of Galilee, be present with you always. *Amen.*

May God the Holy Spirit, who has given you the will to persevere in your love and in your covenant with each other, strengthen your bond. *Amen.*

And may God the Holy Trinity, the source of all unity, bless you this day and for ever. *Amen.*

PRAYERS FOR TODAY'S CHURCH
AND THE BOOK OF OCCASIONAL SERVICES*

•55 Home and Family

O God, who settest the solitary in families, we lift before thee the dear and sacred interests of our homes.
We beseech thee to hear us, O Lord.

Make our families radiant centers of joy and schools of character. Grant to those who are married true love and loyalty; to parents, for their children's sake, the persuasiveness of good and faithful lives; to youth the gladness that has no bitter fruit and integrity that need not be ashamed.
We beseech thee to hear us, O Lord.

Deliver us from the spiritual foes of our households, from mean tempers, and envy of others' goods, from petulant moods and nagging tongues, and

from all loveless and disloyal dealing whereby marriage is despoiled of glory and childhood of its chance.
We beseech thee to hear us, O Lord.

We rejoice in memories of loved ones by whose death heaven becomes more homelike to our imagining. O God, from whom every family in heaven and on earth is named, save us from betraying the great love wherewith our kinsfolk have loved us.
We beseech thee to hear us, O Lord.

For the nation's sake, whose foundations are in the family, we pray for the homes of our people. From marriage vows lightly planned, carelessly made, and trivially broken,
Good Lord, deliver us.

From public evils which impoverish households, degrade childhood, cheapen love, and dishonor old age,
Good Lord, deliver us.

O Christ, who hast called God Father and all thy brothers and sisters, give us thy spirit of good will and fidelity that we may build homes with the shadow of the Almighty for their covering and defense; within their shelter may tranquility abide and joy abound; may Christian faith and fruitful character find there congenial soil; may the world's vulgarity and selfishness cease at their peaceful door; and from them may the zeal of youth and the strength of maturity go forth to make at last the whole earth a home and all humanity one family in thee.
Lord, have mercy upon us and grant us this blessing. Amen.

HARRY EMERSON FOSDICK

• 56 Fathers

Alleluia! happy the man who dreads the Lord
By joyfully keeping the commandments.
Alleluia! He is happy indeed.

Children of such men will be powers on earth,
Descendents of the upright will always be blessed.
Alleluia! He is happy indeed.

Everything will prosper in his family,
For his virtue will never falter.
Alleluia! He is happy indeed.

Giving light to good men in a dark world,

He is merciful, tender-hearted, virtuous.
Alleluia! He is happy indeed.

Interest is not charged by this good man,
Justly he conducts all his business.
Alleluia! He is happy indeed.

Kept safe by virtue, he stands for ever,
Leaving behind him an imperishable memory;
Alleluia! He is happy indeed.

Maintaining his confidence in the Lord,
Never needing to fear bad news,
Alleluia! He is happy indeed.

Outfacing fear with firmness of heart, until
Patience is rewarded by the downfall of enemies.
Alleluia! He is happy indeed.

Quick to be generous, he gives to the poor;
Right conduct for him is no passing fancy.
Alleluia! He is happy indeed.

Such men as this will always be honored,
Though this fills the wicked with fury,
Alleluia! He is happy indeed.

Until, grinding their teeth, they waste away,
Vanishing like their empty aspirations.
Alleluia! Happy the man who dreads the Lord
By joyfully keeping the commandments. Amen.

PSALM 112*

• 57 Mothers

O God of grace and love, we pray for your richest blessing upon all mothers:

Loving God, we thank you that Jesus enjoyed a mother's love and grew up within a family.
Thanks be to God!

We thank you for the homes where we were born and for the care and affection of our mothers.
Thanks be to God!

We thank you if we are still privileged to enjoy the warmth and security of family life.
Thanks be to God!

We pray for all mothers today:

For expectant mothers, especially those awaiting the birth of their first child;
We pray to you, O Lord.

For those who have young children and who get tired and harassed with so much to do;
We pray to you, O Lord.

For those with difficult homes, whose children are more of a problem than a blessing;
We pray to you, O Lord.

For those with difficult husbands, who find it hard to be constant and loving;
We pray to you, O Lord.

For those who find it hard to make ends meet, or who go short themselves for the sake of their families;
We pray to you, O Lord.

For those who are nearly at the end of their tether;
We pray to you, O Lord.

For those who are anxious because their children are growing up and seem to be growing away from them;
We pray to you, O Lord.

For those who feel a sense of emptiness as their children marry and leave home;
We pray to you, O Lord.

For those mothers who are trying to make Christ real to their families;
We pray to you, O Lord.

For those who do not know him as their Savior, nor how to cast their care on him;
We pray to you, O Lord.

For those who are elderly and may feel unwanted;
We pray to you, O Lord.

For those have no husband to share their responsibilities – the widowed, the divorced and the unmarried mother,
We pray to you, O Lord.

We pray also for those who have been denied the privilege of motherhood –
those who cannot have children of their own, and those who have never had
the opportunity to marry,
We pray to you, O Lord.

Lastly, we pray for those closest to us; may we love and care for them as we
ourselves have been loved and helped. We ask it for your love's sake. *Amen.*

CHRISTOPHER IDLE AND JOHN D. SEARLE
–PRAYERS FOR TODAY'S CHURCH

•58 Friendship

O gracious Spirit, who hast tempered the rigor of this present world with the
loveliness of friendship, we rejoice in our friends.
Thanks be to thee, O Lord.

For the encouragement of their love, the support of their confidence, the
faithfulness of their counsel, and the warmth of their affection,
Thanks be to thee, O Lord.

For those most singular and blessed gifts of friendship – power to keep faith
with our own souls; to walk cleanly amid the soil and bravely amid the
disheartenment of life; to believe in our best in the face of failure, and in
extremities to be of excellent hope,
Thanks be to thee, O Lord.

For friends, living on earth and departed hence, whose love has been our
peace and strength; for the beauty of their lives through which thou hast
shined upon us like the sun through eastern windows; and for thy Christ who
called us not servants, but friends,
Thanks be to thee, O Lord.

Because our sins hurt not ourselves only, but our friends, we are ashamed
and penitent. For hasty temper and thoughtless word, for lack of kindliness
and understanding, and for all disloyal dealing, open or secret, whereby we
have betrayed those who trusted us,
We repent before thee, O Lord.

We stand in awe before our power to sway the lives and control the
happiness of those who love us. For all misuse of friendship to untoward
ends, for unbelief that mars the faith of friends, for low tastes which drag
them down, for miserable moods which cloud their skies, and for all
unworthy living which roughens their spiritual journey,
We repent before thee, O Lord.

Because friendship is so excellent a grace, widen its domain, we beseech thee. Reclaim from violence and strife the relationships of races and nations; redeem them from suspicion and prejudice to good will and trust. O Sun of Righteousness, shine on our fierce and wayward world, and lighten its path to closeness and unity in thee.
Lord, have mercy upon us and grant us this blessing.

Make our human friendships, we beseech thee, a revelation to our souls of thine unfailing love. Despite the mysterious dealings of thy Providence, may we walk by faith in thy friendliness. Enfold us in thy grace, support us by thy power, establish us in thy fellowship, and grant us the crown of life, that we should ever be the friends of God.
Lord, have mercy upon us and grant us this blessing. Amen.

HARRY EMERSON FOSDICK

•59 The Various Ages of Life

Leader: We come from the various ages of our lives, Father, offering what we are,

All: *and asking that your love*
will continue,
age after age,
year after year.

A child: Be with your people who are children.
Help their teachers and parents.
Keep them from harm and danger.
Make them strong and wise and happy.

All: *Father, may your love continue with us year after year.*

An elderly person: Be with your people who are old.
Give them patience for their infirmities,
and companions for their lonely hours.
Give them new evidence of your love,
and teach them to trust you
above all others.

All: *Father, may your love continue with us year after year.*

A young person: Be with your people who are young.
Encourage their enthusiasm,
resolve their doubts and anxieties,
and lengthen their perspectives.

All: *Father, may your love continue with us year after year.*

A person
in mid-life: Be with your people in mid-life.
Help them to deal with their fears
for themselves and their families.
Preserve them from boredom,
selfishness and indulgence,
and other bad fruits
of our affluent society.

All: *Father, may your love continue with us year after year.*

Leader: See us in our stages in life, Father,
and come to us in our needs.
Show us how we need each other,
and the ways in which we can come together.

All: *Lord, help us to meet each other's needs.*

A Child: Give those of us who are children
the love of those who might be
our grandparents.
We need the time they can give to us,
and their love.

All: *Lord, help us to meet each other's needs.*

An
elderly
person: Give those of us who are old
young children whom we might spoil
with our love.
We need their smiles and joy,
their innocent view of life.

All: *Lord, help us to meet each other's needs.*

A young
person: Give those of us who are young
the friendship of those who might be
our parents.
We need their interest in our lives,
their counsel and advice.

All: *Lord, help us to meet each other's needs.*

A person
in mid-life: Give those of us who are in mid-life
the young whom we might see
as though seeing ourselves.
We need their carefree confidence,
their newer ways of thinking and doing.

All: *Lord, help us to meet each other's needs.*

Leader: Our times are in your hands, Father,
and a thousand years in your sight
are like a day.
You know that the youngest among us
will become the oldest,
that even the oldest is but a child
before you.

All: *Help us to see what we need from one another,*
and how we can help one another,
after the example of Jesus Christ, your Son, our Lord,
who lives and reigns with you
and the Holy Spirit,
one God now and for ever. Amen.

CARL T. UEHLING

•60 On Growing Old

Holy Trinity, One God,
Gateway to eternity,
Help us to your kingdom.

Lord,
Our thoughts are as hard to communicate
As they were when we were children.
We talk,
Sometimes endlessly, we fear,
And the expressions on the faces of listeners
Show that they do not hear.
Preoccupied,
They wait to leave us.
Holy Trinity, One God,
Gateway to eternity,
Reunite us in your kingdom.

But it need not be a sorrow
To find ourselves alone.
We need some time
To rearrange our memories
And discard mistaken choices,
So that what we keep
To bring to you
May be named the best we knew.

Holy Trinity, One God,
Gateway to eternity,
Perfect us for your kingdom.

And yet,
Our losses we recall with pain.
With the ache in our bones
Comes an aching longing
To hear again a familiar laugh,
To feel the tenderness,
To share.
Lord, save us from living on memory.
You have the company of those we loved.
You share it now.
To be old is to miss those with whom we learned our sharing.
Holy Trinity, One God,
Gateway to eternity,
Fill us with longing for your kingdom.

Still, Lord, we must not
Neglect the present.
Today may be the last we have
To enjoy
The manner in which morning sunlight comes,
And evening shadows lengthen;
To smile at friends;
To read a printed page,
Let some wisdom
We did not know before
Strike at our hearts with
leaping recognition.
Yes!
Holy Trinity, One God,
Gateway to eternity,
Prepare us for your kingdom.

Tonight our souls may be required of us.
Holy Trinity, One God,
Gateway to eternity,
Welcome us to your kingdom.
Amen.

KAY SMALLZRIED

Teachers and Students

•61 For Leaders and Teachers

Reader 1: Now there was a leader of the Pharisees named Nicodemus, a member of the Jewish council. This man came to Jesus by night and said to him, "Rabbi, we know that you are a teacher sent by God; for no one can do these signs that you are doing unless God is with him."

Reader 2: Jesus was prepared for his work . . .
By prayer, by worship, by study,
by all things that we experience
we are prepared for our work.

All: *God, grant us the desire and the will*
to prepare for this great task of ours.

Reader 1: Jesus understood those he was teaching . . .

Reader 2: Jesus adapted his teaching to the individuals concerned.
Jesus treated everyone with respect and understanding.

All: *God, grant us humble hearts,*
that we may come more and more
to understand ourselves and others
even as all are understood by you.

Reader 1: Jesus was patient . . .

Reader 2: Jesus, God of God, Light of Light, very God of very God, exercised patience when his soul must have burned with impatience to get on with, and to accomplish, the work that had to be done.

All: *God, grant us the grace*
to restrain ourselves with patience.

Reader 1: Jesus was filled with compassion when he saw the great throng, because they were like sheep without a shepherd; and he began to teach them many things.

Reader 2: Put on, then, as God's chosen ones, holy and beloved, compassion, kindness, lowliness, meekness, and patience, forbearing one another in love.

All: *God, grant us that holy compassion*
which fills the Christian life
with a restless yearning to minister to others
in their need.

Reader 1: Jesus was calm and not hurried . . .

Reader 2: His self-control and naturalness in every incident are evidences of strength. His calmness stands in striking contrast to the perturbed confusion of the disciples in times of stress.

All: *God, grant us the gift*
of a calm, unhurried life.
Let us work without haste, and yet with diligence,
and so give glory to your Name.

Reader 1: Jesus used everyday matters and incidents as a means of teaching . . .

Reader 2: Jesus took what was at hand, and the experience of the people, and used it for his purposes.

All: *God, grant us the ability*
to see in all of life
a means of teaching and leading,
and a revelation of who you are, and who we are.

Reader 1: And finally, let us all rejoice
if in all our efforts,
in all our praying,
in all our days,
there is one person who says,

Reader 2: "We know that you are a teacher sent by God."

(Silence)

103

All: *O God, sustain your Church*
as we face new tasks in the confusions of this changing world.
By your Holy Spirit
give us good judgement and the strength to persevere,
so that we may boldly bear witness
to the coming of your kingdom;
through Jesus Christ our Lord.
Amen.

ADAPTED BY JEFFERY W. ROWTHORN

•62 For Those Who Teach

Leader: St. Paul wrote: "If it is teaching, let us give all that we have to our teaching."

Jesus said, "Whoever among you wants to be great must become the servant of all; for the Son of Man himself has not come to be served, but to serve."

Teachers: *Our purpose is not to become the God of the classroom,*
Nor to make our class the pride of the school,
Nor to make our school the showcase of the city.
We serve children because they will grow into adults;
Because their minds and spirits are hungry,
We shall feed them.

Leader: Jesus said, "I am come that they may have life."

Teachers: *We teach for their sake, that they may know God's world;*
Knowing, that they may delight and worship in it;
Delighting, that their lives may find free service and full expression in it.

Leader: Jesus was born in a borrowed crib, accepted friendship from his disciples, ointment from Mary, and the Cross from his enemies. All these he touched with a new glory.

Teachers: *Our selves and our gifts we offer for his service.*
We do not want to be envious of the talents of our colleagues,
But to be glad about our own gifts.
Accept and glorify our gifts, O Lord.

Leader: Jesus said that happiness belonged to the humble-minded, the meek, the merciful, the sincere, those hungry and thirsty for goodness.

Teachers:	*Let us share this happiness,*
	By reassessing ourselves and our work, and by being ready to alter what is wrong;
	By learning from the experience and character of other people;
	By co-operating freely with those in authority over us, remembering the particular responsibilities they always bear;
	By having the grace to be open to advice and, if necessary, correction from those under us.

Leader: Jesus had all things committed to him by the Father, but wrapped himself with a towel and washed the feet of the disciples.

Teachers: *Help us, O Lord, to accept the mundane things that sometimes gall our spirits: duties at lunchtime or recess; extra work for a sick colleague or a student teacher; visits by inspectors and health workers.*

Leader: Jesus welcomed children with their mothers and blessed them. He said, "Let them come, for of such is the Kingdom of heaven."

Teachers: *Grant that we may share your compassion, Lord, and therefore your patience with awkward children or difficult parents.*

Leader: Jesus said, "My peace I give to you".

Teachers: *Enable us to work from your peace;*
To have confidence for the moment, and not hunger restlessly for results;
To give each hour its full value as part of the whole education of the child;
And when the day ends with frayed nerves, still to be wise in the use of time and temper.

Leader: Jesus, you say to us, "Come, follow me";

Teachers: *Keep us, through the Holy Spirit's work, in the thrill and awe of our calling, for the sake of your Kingdom.*
Amen.

FRANK GODFREY
–WORSHIP FOR TODAY

•63 Students Around the World

Let us pray for the students of the world.

(Silence)

For those who are persecuted and imprisoned for their faith,
Lord, hear and help.

For those who live in constant fear,
Lord, hear and help.

For those who are ill or hungry or cold,
Lord, hear and help.

For those who are in despair at the collapse of false hopes,
Lord, hear and help.

For those who are blinded by this world's success, that they may come to know the love of God,
Lord, hear and help.

For those who are lonely, that they may find comfort in the Gospel,
Lord, hear and help.

(Silence)

Let us pray for those in revolutionary situations, that they may confess their faith in the hour of trial and show forth a true picture of community in Christ,
Lord, hear and help.

For those in newly independent countries, that they may seize with zeal the great opportunities open to them to bring their people closer together,
Lord, hear and help.

For those who have civil strife raging in their countries, that they may be comforted in the face of the terrors surrounding them, and thereby be strengthened to comfort others by word and deed,
Lord, hear and help.

(Silence)

Let us pray for those of us who find our work too difficult,
Lord, hear and help.

For those who do not give of their best in their work,
Lord, hear and help.

For those who are oppressed by the fear of failure in examinations,
Lord, hear and help.

Young people who, seeking emancipation, have entered a new bondage to unworthy thinking or behaving, obedient to group pressures which they would not have heeded at the first,
Our prayer and our caring, O God, hold up to you.

Those who seek to pray and cannot, seek to live by your Word, yet find it closed to them, seek to control their appetites but are controlled by them, seek to use their minds to the fullest but find they cannot study,
Our prayer and our caring, O God, hold up to you.

Those about us who, finding the faulty foundations of their Christian faith destroyed, disavow it or grope in disillusion for some great purpose to take its place in their lives,
Our prayer and our caring, O God, hold up to you.

Chaplains and leaders of the life of the Spirit among students or faculty, that they may be strong, quick-thinking, never apologetic and never dull, brave to declare Christian truth amid the attractions of materialism and the eager preoccupations of secular life,
Our prayer and our caring, O God, hold up to you.

Lord Jesus Christ, whom the people called Teacher, knowledge of your truth has set people at liberty in every generation. Grant us the grace to be faithful when we are surrounded with attractive unbelief, the humility to be trustful among genteel scoffers, the staying power of Christian commitment even when doubt seems most reasonable. So may we endure as seeing him who is invisible, even our strong Savior Jesus Christ. *Amen.*

JOHN OLIVER NELSON
–THE STUDENT PRAYER BOOK

•65 The Young

Let us give thanks for Christ's revelation to us of God's love for children and of their infinite value in God's sight;
We thank you, O Lord.

For Christ's tender compassion towards them; for his burning indignation against those who do them wrong; for this deep and overflowing love, drawing them with irresistible attraction to himself; for his message of their nearness to the Father of all;
We thank you, O Lord.

For the beauty of children and their joy in all beautiful things, for their merriment and laughter, and for the joy and light they bring into the world;

We thank you, O Lord.

For their enthusiasm, their abounding energy, and their love of the heroic and adventurous; for their candid, generous trust in those around them, and for their quick response to calls of love and service;
We thank you, O Lord.

O Lord, forgive because there are still children in need of care and love;
O Lord, forgive.

Because homes are broken by selfishness, pride and greed,
O Lord, forgive.

Because, even in our affluence, children remain in great spiritual and moral danger,
O Lord, forgive.

Because children continue to be exploited by the greedy and the lustful,
O Lord, forgive.

Because children in many parts of the world suffer from disease and malnutrition,
O Lord, forgive.

Because many children are homeless and many are not taught to read or write,
O Lord, forgive.

Because many children live in fear, and have not heard the good news of Jesus Christ,
O Lord, forgive.

Because these great needs cannot always be met for want of skilled workers and adequate resources,
O Lord, forgive.

(Silence)

O Lord God, forgive what we have been, sanctify what we are, direct what we shall be; for Jesus Christ's sake. Amen.

THE ANGLICAN CATHEDRAL, LIVERPOOL
–PRAYERS FOR TODAY'S CHURCH

•66 Litany for Youth

All: *O God, we are your children; help us to know that we are*
        never forgotten, never deserted, always forgiven, always loved.

Leader 1:   O God, we have meant to serve you better than we do, but
        we have not.

Leader 2:   We have dreamed dreams of all that we would do for you,
        and we have seldom even started.

All: *O God, we are your children; help us to know that we are*
        never forgotten, never deserted, always forgiven, always loved.

Leader 1:   O God, the whole world lies before us. We have many
        choices, and we are often confused.

Leader 2:   Help us to choose wisely those things that will affect all our
        lives – the things we study, the people we marry, the work
        we do.

All: *O God, we are your children; help us to know that we are*
        never forgotten, never deserted, always forgiven, always loved.

Leader 1:   O God, we know that you are greater than we can imagine.
        We know that we were made in your image. But we think
        small thoughts of you and big thoughts of ourselves.

Leader 2:   Help us to know you as that Spirit which reaches from the
        smallest blade of grass to the farthest star; that Love which
        is so great that it leans down from heaven to help us in our
        every action.

All: *O God, we are your children; help us to know that we are*
        never forgotten, never deserted, always forgiven, always loved.

Leader 1:   O God, we know that you are not just the God of our
        denomination, our country, our friends and family, but we
        find it hard to act as if we really believed it.

Leader 2:   We say that all people are brothers and sisters, but we forget
        that members of one family are often very different. We try
        to ignore the differences in our customs and beliefs. Help us
        to understand them instead of pretending they don't exist,
        and to respect all ways of worshipping and serving you.

All: *O God, we are your children; help us to know that we are*
        never forgotten, never deserted, always forgiven, always loved.

Leader 1: O God, we find fault with Christianity without ever really trying it. We lose our tempers over customs that seem old-fashioned and neglect the truth hidden under them.

Leader 2: O Father, help us to know that you made us and all the world, and that you love your creation.

Leader 1: O Christ, help us to know that you came to us because we have not the strength to go to you, and that you come to us still.

Leader 2: O Holy Spirit, help us to know that you are within each one of us, ready to teach if we are ready to learn.

All: *O God, we are your children; help us to know that we are never forgotten, never deserted, always forgiven, always loved.*

Leader 1: O God, we know that you are not just in church, in saintly people or in great actions, but we forget.

Leader 2: Help us to see you in our enemies as well as in our friends.

Leader 1: Help us to be patient with our families when they do not understand us, to learn to look for things to love in unattractive people, to forgive those who hurt us and to ask forgiveness when we hurt others.

Leader 2: Help us to laugh at ourselves and so begin to learn humility. Help us to praise you in everything we do, and for everyone we meet.

All: *O God, we are your children; help us to know that we are never forgotten, never deserted, always forgiven, always loved.*

Leader 1: O God, we want peace and we are very afraid. We are afraid of pain and terror, of war and chaos and things we have not known.

Leader 2: We are afraid, too, of little things, of being thought foolish and laughed at, of having those we love think badly of us, of failing some test the world has set us, but we do not fear you, God, nor trust you very much, because you are not real enough to us.

All: *O God, we are your children; help us to know that we are never forgotten, never deserted, always forgiven, always loved.*

Leader 1: O God, help us to learn to know you, to know that you were at our beginning and will be at our end, that you call to us now and will call through whatever comes to us all our lives long.

Leader 2: O Christ, our friend as well as our judge, our companion in temptation, in suffering and in love, help us to know you and to love you by walking in the path that you have made for us.

All: *O God, we are your children; help us to know that we are never forgotten, never deserted, always forgiven, always loved.*

Leader 1: O God, take us by the hand and forgive us when we fall;

Leader 2: Lift us up and help us to try again.

All: *O Father, strengthen us;*
O Christ, walk with us;
O Holy Spirit, teach us;
for we are your children,
never forgotten, never deserted,
always forgiven, always loved.
Amen.

AVERY BROOKE

•67 The Right Time to Be Different

God of wisdom, help us to know the right time to be different.

As Noah ignored the laughter of the world,
may we follow your will in spite of ridicule.

As Joseph resisted the invitation of Potiphar's wife,
may we control the power of sex in our lives.

As Daniel risked his life for the right to worship,
may we grow day by day in our personal devotion.

As Amos fearlessly pointed to the sins and failures of his time,
may we speak for rightness, justice, and love.

As David accepted the challenge all others shunned,
may we meet the fearful decisions of life.

As Elizabeth's baby leaped for joy at the coming of the Lord,
may we find excitement in your nearness.

As Mary kept those things and pondered them in her heart,
may we take time to meditate on your love.

As Stephen prayed for those who stoned him,
may we learn the virtue of a forgiving heart.

As Peter was taught not to call anything unclean that you have made clean,
may we conquer prejudice and hatred for your sake.

As Paul responded eagerly to the battle of the Christian life,
may we willingly walk in the Spirit.

As the Son of Man came not to be served but to serve,
*may we give of our life and time and money for the physical and spiritual good
of others.*
Amen.

ELMER N. WITT
–TIME TO PRAY

•68 At a High School Baccalaureate

*Each section may be used separately, or the whole may be used as one continuous
litany.*

Leader 1:   Lord, it is your will for us to welcome new freedoms.

Leader 2:   We welcome new freedom to embark on a career,
freedom to earn our own money, or train
to earn it,
freedom to spend our money, or save it,
freedom to fashion new routines,
freedom to plan leisure,
freedom to bear new responsibilities,
freedom to make fresh meaning out of life.

Leader 1:   We welcome new freedom to grow into the world you have
given us,
to travel to the destination you have
prepared for us,
to meet and serve the people you have
waiting for us.

Leader 2:   In the challenge of freedom

Graduates: *Equip us.*

114

Leader 1:	In the decisions of freedom
Graduates:	*Direct us.*
Leader 2:	In the art of freedom
Graduates:	*Discipline us.*
Leader 1:	In the dangers of freedom
Graduates:	*Protect us.*
Leader 2:	In the raptures of freedom
Graduates:	*Steady us.*
Leader 1:	In the life of freedom
Graduates:	*Give us joy.*
Leader 2:	In the use of freedom
Graduates:	*Grant us wisdom.*

Leader 1: What a world!
21 million people killed in one war.
Everyone still at a loss to know how to turn enemies into friends and to free their way of life from the thread of nuclear disaster.
Two-thirds of the world kept hungry.
Thousands killed every year on the roads.

Leader 2: Now it is our turn, and we shall be responsible too.

Leader 1: To bear this responsibility we shall need your protection, Lord – the armor-plating of your Spirit. O Lord, protect us.

Leader 2: Protect us from big business which sees us as industrial fodder.

Graduates: *Yes, Lord, protect us.*

Leader 1: From slick salesmen who treat us as an easy market for industrial junk,

Graduates: *Yes, Lord, protect us.*

Leader 2: From glib advertisements that promise success for the price of a tube of toothpaste,

Graduates: *Yes, Lord, protect us.*

Leader 1: From the pressure of unscrupulous competition, from status symbols and lust for money and position,

Graduates:	*Yes, Lord, protect us.*
Leader 2:	From those who would foul our minds, soil our bodies, and ignore our spirits,
Graduates:	*Yes, Lord, protect us.*
Leader 1:	From the bomb, the bottle, the drug, and the car crash,
Graduates:	*Yes, Lord, protect us.*
Leader 2:	From ourselves, for we are often our worst enemy,
Graduates:	*Yes, Lord, protect us.*
Leader 1:	The Son has set us free,
Graduates:	*And we are free indeed.*
Leader 2:	What, free to stand the relentless din and monotony of the factory?
Graduates:	*Yes, but not to be dehumanized by it.*
Leader 1:	What, free to take interminable exams?
Graduates:	*Yes, but not to be victimized by them.*
Leader 2:	What, free to be involved in the sins of humanity?
Graduates:	*Yes, but to be forgiven by the One on whom they fall.*
Leader 1:	What, free to believe in a God of love in a world of ruin?
Graduates:	*Yes, but not without proving him true.*
Leader 2:	What, free to die?
Graduates:	*Yes, but only to find we are sons and daughters of God, and meant for eternity.*
Leader 1:	Against all the victimization of the world,
Graduates:	*the Son has set us free, and we are free indeed.*
Leader 2:	So in the freedom of the Son,

Graduates: *we shall make money honestly,*
we shall make love honorably,
we shall make time for those who need us,
we shall make friends of our enemies,
we shall make amends straight away,
we shall make God supreme,
for God's service in the world is perfect freedom.
Amen.

PAUL KIMBER AND OTHERS
–WORSHIP FOR TODAY

•69 God of the World Around Us

Leader and People:

God of concrete, God of steel,
God of piston and of wheel,
God of pylon, God of steam,
God of girder and of beam,
God of atom, God of mine,
All the world of power is Thine!

Leader:
O God our Father,
We praise you because we see you in the wonders of this universe – in the
life-giving sun by day, in the moon and the galaxies of stars by night, in the
immensities of space and the beauty of nature and the marvels of energy;
We acknowledge you and praise you as the Lord of all creation.

We praise you because we see you in the development of humanity, the
growth of nations and the movements of peoples;
We acknowledge you and praise you as the Lord of all history.

God of Turk and God of Greek,
God of ev'ry tongue we speak,
God of Arab, God of Jew,
God of ev'ry race and hue,
God who knows no bound'ry line,
All the world of men is Thine!

We praise you because we see you leading people to discover the meaning
and purpose of existence;
We acknowledge you and praise you as the Lord of truth and life.

117

We praise you because we seek you at work in men and women who put to good use the raw material of creation, who experiment, plant, and build, who manufacture, produce and use all that is entrusted to us;
We acknowledge you and praise you as the Lord of agriculture and industry.

> *Lord of science, Lord of art,*
>> *Lord of map and graph and chart,*
> *Lord of physics and research,*
>> *Word of Bible, Faith of Church,*
> *Lord of sequence and design*
>> *All the world of truth is Thine!*

We praise you because we see you incarnate and revealed in Jesus, the carpenter of Nazareth, in whom all human labor is made sacred;
We acknowledge you and praise you as the Lord of all work.

We praise you because we see you helping people to be in contact with one another and to transport to one another the products of their work;
We acknowledge you and praise you as the Lord of communications and trade.

> *Lord of cable, Lord of rail,*
>> *Lord of interstate and mail,*
> *Lord of rocket, Lord of flight,*
>> *Lord of soaring satellite,*
> *Lord of lightning's vivid line,*
>> *All the world of speed is Thine!*

We praise you because we see you cooperating with people in their work, seeking to make things of true value, reconciling differences between management and workers, and bringing peace to the world of industry;
We acknowledge you and praise you as the Lord of reconciliation.

We praise you because we see condemned on the Cross, on which Jesus was killed, selfishness, pride, the avoidance of responsibility, hard-heartedness and cowardice; and see exalted, as the one hope of all, the love that seeks to save and be spent in the service of others, the love that sacrifices, the love that unites, and the love that conquers.
We acknowledge you and praise you as the source and Lord of love.

> *God whose glory fills the earth,*
>> *Gave the universe its birth,*
> *Loosed the Christ with Easter's might,*
>> *Saves the world from evil's blight,*
> *Claims us all by grace divine,*
>> *All the world of love is Thine!*

WORSHIP FOR TODAY
HYMN STANZAS BY RICHARD G. JONES*

•70 For Those Who Work

O Lord God: you are ever at work in the world for us and for all humankind.
Guide and protect all who work to get their living.
Amen.

For those who plow the earth,
For those who tend machinery;
Work with them, O God.

For those who sail deep waters,
For those who venture into space;
Work with them, O God.

For those who work in offices and warehouses,
For those who labor in stores or factories;
Work with them, O God.

For those who work in mines,
For those who buy and sell;
Work with them, O God.

For those who entertain us,
For those who broadcast or publish;
Work with them, O God.

For those who keep house,
For those who train children;
Work with them, O God.

For all who live by strength of arm,
For all who live by skill of hand;
Work with them, O God.

For all who employ or govern;
Work with them, O God.

For all who excite our minds with art, science, or learning;
Work with them, O God.

For all who instruct,
For writers and teachers;
Work with them, O God.

For all who serve the public good in any way by working;
Work with them, O God.

For all who labor without hope,
For all who labor without interest;
Great God: we pray your mercy, grace, and saving power.

For those who have too little leisure,
For those who have too much leisure;
Great God: we pray your mercy, grace, and saving power.

For those who are underpaid,
For those who pay small wages;
Great God: we pray your mercy, grace, and saving power.

For those who cannot work,
For those who look in vain for work;
Great God: we pray your mercy, grace, and saving power.

For those who trade on the troubles of others,
For profiteers, extortioners, and greedy people;
Great God: we pray your mercy, grace, and saving power.

Work through us and help us always to work for you; in Jesus Christ our Lord.
Amen.

THE WORSHIPBOOK

•71 For All Workers

O God, you have made us a royal priesthood, that we might offer to you prayer and intercession for people of every sort and condition; hear us as we pray.

For all who toil in the burden and the heat of day, that they may enjoy the rewards of their industry, that they may not be defrauded of their due, and that we may never cease to be mindful of our debt to them, remembering with gratitude the multitude of services which must be performed to make our life tolerable:
We pray your grace and pledge our concern, O God.

For those who have authority and power over their fellows, that they may not use it for selfish advantage, but be guided to do justice and to love mercy:
We pray your grace and pledge our concern, O God.

For those who have been wounded in the battles of life, whether by the inhumanity of their fellows, their own limitations, or the fickleness of fortune, that they may contend against injustice without bitterness, overcome their own weakness with diligence, and learn how to accept with patience what cannot be altered:
We pray your grace and pledge our concern, O God.

For the rulers of the nations, that they may act wisely and without pride, may seek to promote peace among the peoples, and establish justice in our common life:
We pray your grace and pledge our concern, O God.

For teachers and ministers of the Word, for artists and interpreters of our spiritual life, that they may rightly divide the word of truth, and not be tempted by pride or greed or any ignoble passion to corrupt the truth to which they are committed:
We pray your grace and pledge our concern, O God.

For prophets and seers and saints, who awaken us from our sloth, that they may continue to hold their torches high in a world darkened by prejudice and sin, and ever be obedient to the heavenly vision:
We pray your grace and pledge our concern, O God.

O Lord, you have bound us together in this bundle of life, give us grace to understand how our lives depend upon the courage, the industry, the honesty and integrity of our fellows; that we may be mindful of their needs, grateful for their faithfulness, and faithful in our responsibilities to them; through Jesus Christ our Lord.
Amen.

REINHOLD NIEBUHR
–WITH ONE VOICE

•72 The Search for Truth

Eternal God, who hast promised us the liberty which follows after truth; grant that, keeping the commandments of Christ, we may have the mind of Christ and be free, as he was free.

For all who guard the truths which were known of old, that, as good stewards of that knowledge, they may confirm us in simple and righteous living;
We beseech thee to hear us, good Lord.

For those who seek for new truth, that, believing more light is yet to break, they may be sustained in their searching by the faith that thou art, and that thou art the rewarder of them that diligently seek thee;
We beseech thee to hear us, good Lord.

For all scientists, looking upon the face of nature, that they may see order in its variety and law in its constancy, and may teach us all to live upon earth in confidence and without fear;

We beseech thee to hear us, good Lord.

For all historians, that, telling again the story of the past with sincerity and sympathy, they may bind the generations together in one communion of thy true children;
We beseech thee to hear us, good Lord.

For all builders, poets, painters, and makers of music, that they may open our blind eyes and unstop our deaf ears to the beauty of thy world;
We beseech thee to hear us, good Lord.

For all who would lead our long thoughts beyond the things that are known into the world which is unknown, that their faith may prepare us for a place in the infinite mystery;
We beseech thee to hear us, good Lord.

For all who unselfishly bring their knowledge to the service of the world, that they may prove their learning by their works, and give that vision without which the people perish;
We beseech thee to hear us, good Lord.

For ourselves, that, seeing clearly and feeling deeply, we may go forth to be in the world as those who serve, and may thus know that mind of Christ which we would make the manner of our thinking;
We beseech thee to hear us, good Lord.

All these things we ask in the Name of Jesus Christ our Lord.
Amen.

WILLARD SPERRY
–WITH ONE VOICE

•73 Our Daily Work

Let us remember that God's first recorded command was to work. Let us ask God's forgiveness for the times when we have considered our work as drudgery rather than as a gift from God.
Lord, in your mercy:
Hear our prayer.

Let us pray for all employers that they may carry out their responsibilities with justice and integrity. Let us pray for the members of this congregation who are employers.
Lord, in your mercy:
Hear our prayer.

Let us pray for all employees that they may do good and honest work. Let us pray for the members of this congregation who are employed by others.
Lord, in your mercy:
Hear our prayer.

Let us pray for the unions, thanking God for all that has been achieved in getting better working conditions and fairer wages for workers. Let us pray for union leaders and shop stewards that they may exercise their great powers wisely and responsibly.
Lord, in your mercy:
Hear our prayer.

Let us pray for those with whom we have relationships through their work or through ours. Let us pray for our colleagues at work and for due appreciation of those who serve us week by week.
Lord, in your mercy:
Hear our prayer.

Let us pray for those whose work is dull and monotonous; for those whose work is dangerous; for those whose work causes them to be separated from their families for long periods; and for those whose work brings them into situations where they are greatly tempted.
Lord, in your mercy:
Hear our prayer.

Let us pray for those who cannot work; for those who cannot find employment; for those who cannot obtain work because they are discriminated against; for those who are disabled; and for those who have retired.
Lord, in your mercy:
Hear our prayer.
Amen.

PRAYERS FOR TODAY'S CHURCH

•74 For the Unemployed

Lord God, have mercy on us for our ignorance and greed which have brought to millions unemployment in the midst of plenty.

From any sense of our own virtue at some gesture of charity to the unemployed,
Good Lord, deliver us.

From luxury and display, while many have nowhere to lay their heads,

Good Lord, deliver us.

From heedless comfort in the security of our homes, while families of the poor are evicted from their homes, their children and furniture upon the street,
Good Lord, deliver us.

From methods of private or public relief which save the bodies of men and women but destroy their inmost spirit; from hurting the finer sensibilities of those in need, robbing them of their pride and self-respect,
Good Lord, deliver us.

From false notions that by preaching we can save people's souls, while unemployment breaks their hearts, unbalances their minds, destroys their homes, tempts them beyond measure, visits want and disease upon their children, turns their heart to bitterness, hatred, and rebellion, or to hopelessness, despair, and death,
Good Lord, deliver us.

From ever forgetting the forlorn figure of the unemployed, and from failure to see that our social fabric is as shabby as their clothes,
Good Lord, deliver us.

From satisfaction with any revival of trade or renewed prosperity while multitudes still can find no work,
Good Lord, deliver us.

That our conscience may know no rest until unemployment is abolished,
We entreat you, good Lord.

That you will guide us quickly to that good life in which there shall be peace and a generous sharing in labor, leisure and joy by all your children,
We entreat you, good Lord.

(Silence)

O God, the Lord of the vineyard, you do not wish any to stand idle in the marketplace; hear our prayer for the multitudes without employment or assurance of livelihood, and in your loving wisdom show us the right ways to help and heal all our distress; through Jesus Christ our Lord.
Amen.

THE STUDENT PRAYER BOOK

•75 With People at Work

When I work with people today, Lord, when I'm inclined to be short-tempered, ill-mannered, inconsiderate of their problems, when I ignore people who are not important to me and forget even to learn their names, *Strengthen me in your way, Lord.*

When I should be a good leader for those under me and a good follower for those over me, *Strengthen me in your way, Lord.*

When I'm inclined to take it easy rather than to work, to extend the social minutes of the day into social hours, to put off rather than to do, *Strengthen me in your way, Lord.*

When I have to make important decisions, *Strengthen me in your way, Lord.*

When I let my affairs slip into confusion and my working hours into disarray, *Strengthen me in your way, Lord.*

When I begin something worthwhile and need help in finishing it, and when I'm tempted to let a good task slip away because it has become difficult, *Strengthen me in your way, Lord.*

When the work week is done, Lord, let me have a good sense of recreation. Let me exercise my body as well as my mind in refreshing pursuits that will return me to my work renewed and fit. In work and play, *Strengthen me in your way, Lord.*
Amen.

HERBERT B. WEST

•76 Litany of the Sundial

Thou who hast put the times and seasons in thine own power:
Grant that we make our prayer unto thee in a time when thou mayest be found, and save us.

Thou who for us and for our salvation was born at dead of night:
Give us daily to be born again by renewing of the Holy Ghost, till Christ be perfectly formed in us, and save us.

Thou who very early in the morning while the sun was yet arising didst rise from the dead:
Raise us up daily unto newness of life,
and save us.

Thou who at the third hour didst send down thy Holy Ghost on the apostles:
Take not away the same Spirit from us, but renew him daily within us,
and save us.

Thou who at the sixth hour didst nail the sins of the world with thyself on the cross:
Blot out the handwriting of our sins which is against us and take it out of the way,
and save us.

Thou who at the seventh hour didst will that the fever should leave the nobleman's son:
If aught abide of fever or of sickness in our soul, take it away from us also,
and save us.

Thou who at the ninth hour for us sinners and for our sins didst taste of death:
Mortify in us whatsoever is contrary to thy will,
and save us.

Thou who at the tenth hour didst will thine apostle, when he found thy Son, to declare with great joy, "We have found the Messiah":
Make us in like sort to find the Messiah, and when he is found, in like sort to rejoice,
and save us.

Thou who at eventide didst will to be taken down from the cross and buried in a tomb:
Bury our sins in thy sepulcher, covering with good works whatsoever we have committed ill,
and save us.

Thou who didst vouchsafe even at the eleventh hour of the day to send men into thy vineyard and to fix a wage, notwithstanding they had stood all day idle:
Do unto us like favor and, though it be late, accept us graciously when we return to thee,
and save us.

Thou who at the hour of supper didst will to institute the most sacred mysteries of the body and blood:
Make us mindful of the same and partakers thereof,
and save us.

Thou who late in the night didst by thy breathing confer on thine apostles the authority as well to forgive as to retain sins:
Make us partakers of that authority, yet that it be unto remission, not unto retention, O Lord,
and save us.

Thou who at midnight didst awaken David thy prophet and Paul the apostle to praise thee:
Give us also songs by night and to remember thee upon our beds,
and save us.

Thou who with thine own mouth hast vouched that at midnight the Bridegroom shall come:
Grant that the cry, "The Bridegroom cometh," may sound evermore in our ears, that we be never unprepared to meet him,
and save us.

Thou who by the crowing of a cock didst admonish thine apostle and make him to return to penitence:
Grant us also at the same admonition to do the same and weep bitterly the things wherein we have sinned against thee,
and save us.

Thou who hast foretold that thou wilt come to judgment in a day when we look not for thee and at an hour when we are not aware:
Make us prepared every day and every hour to be ready for thine advent,
and save us.
Amen.

LANCELOT ANDREWES

•77 For Farmers and Their Families

Let us give thanks to God:

For the wonder of the changing seasons and the ever-new miracle of life stirring in field and forest,
We give you thanks, O God.

For the privilege of sharing with you in the act of creating the good things of earth for your children, and for your nearness in all the phases of agricultural life,
We give you thanks, O God.

For the Christ of the country road, who walked and served in the countryside of Galilee, and who today walks the backroads of the world in comradeship with those who till the soil,
We give you thanks, O God.

For the coming of seed-time, for good soil, for abundant rains,
We give you thanks, O God.

For the friendship which prompts farmers to share tools and labor,
We give you thanks, O God.

For neighbors who help when sickness or death, old age or new life come to us,
We give you thanks, O God.

For better seeds, better methods, county agents and other helps to us who farm the land,
We give you thanks, O God.

For the Grange and other community associations,
We give you thanks, O God.

For the blessings of sleep and the renewed strengh of awakening in the morning,
We give you thanks, O God.

That you will grant us a vision of the earth redeemed and used as a sacred trust for the welfare of all your great family on earth,
We ask you to hear us, O Lord.

That you will give us skill in planting and tending our crops and caring for our herds,
We ask you to hear us, O Lord.

That you will give us strength and health and knowledge of your laws so that our bodies may be useful in your service,
We ask you to hear us, O Lord.

That you will bless the rural churches of the world and their ministers, that their fellowship may be enriched and that they may bring their neighbors into lasting fellowship with you,
We ask you to hear us, O Lord.

That you will speedily grant a just and lasting peace in all the earth, that people everywhere may again beat their swords into plowshares and their spears into pruning-hooks, and all live together in harmony and tranquility in the lands you have given them,
We ask you to hear us, O Lord.

That all may share with joy in sowing the seed and reaping the harvest of the
Kingdom of God,
We dedicate our hands and our minds, O God.

To a renewed appreciation of the holy earth and its gifts, and to a
consecrated stewardship of all its resources, material and human,
We dedicate our hands and our minds, O Lord.

To comradeship with the rural peoples of the world, and to sharing with
them generously all the gifts and graces you have given us,
We dedicate our skills and our lives, O God.

Accept our thanks,
hear our prayers,
and graciously use the gifts of mind, body, and soul
which we now lay upon your altar,
through Jesus Christ our Lord.
Amen.

RURAL PEOPLE AT WORSHIP

•78 The Dedication of Life and Labor

Leader: We are now assembled for the purpose of dedicating soil that
is cultivated, seed that is planted, tools that are used on the
land, machines from our factories, the equipment of our
offices, and the men and women who labor in the service of
God and for the good of all.

First
Speaker: Soil we bring to you, O Lord.

Leader: May the Lord teach us to use and conserve this soil and
work to increase its fertility year by year.

Second
Speaker: Seed we bring to you, O Lord.

Leader: May the Lord bless this seed, and cause it to bring forth
food for the men and women and children of our land.

Third
Speaker: Our tools and machines we lay at your feet, O Lord.

Leader: May the Lord strengthen us to use these implements – hoe,
plow and tractor, and the machines in our factories which
grind and bake, process and can our daily food.

Fourth
Speaker: Our typewriters and ledgers we offer to you, O Lord.

Leader: May the Lord help us to plan, account and record, and do
            our business honestly, accurately, and justly.

All: *We come before you, O Lord,*
            as representatives of the workers of this world –
            farmers, machine operators, drivers, clerks, accountants and
            *   executives –*
            and we dedicate ourselves and our work to you.

Leader: May the Lord bless you as you work with him, whatever
            your work may be. Acknowledge your responsibilities;
            cultivate the soil with care and save it from erosion; handle
            your tools and machines with respect and keep them
            serviced; drive with care and courtesy and deliver your
            loads; let integrity, right relationships, and an understanding
            of one another's problems and needs seal all your duties.

            Let us pray
            That men and women may increasingly work together for the
            good of all and for the welfare of the whole community.

All::   *This we ask of you, good Lord.*

Leader: That the rich resources of the earth may be used to do away
            with hunger and malnutrition and bring health and strength
            to all people.

All: *This we ask of you, good Lord.*

Leader: That the towns and cities, as well as farmland and
            countryside, may be places of beauty and free from ugliness,
            squalor and disease.

All: *This we ask of you, good Lord.*

Leader: That God will accept the offering of the worlds of
            agriculture, industry, and commerce, and help us to work as
            fellow laborers with him.

All: *All this we pray through Jesus Christ our Lord.*
            Amen.

MICHAEL APPLEYARD AND OTHERS
–WORSHIP FOR TODAY

•79 The Presentation of Gifts at Harvest Time

Minister: Let us with gladness present the offerings and oblations of our life and labor to the Lord.

All: *Let us with a gladsome mind*
Praise the Lord, for he is kind;
For his mercies aye endure,
Ever faithful, ever sure.

The Gift of Bread *(Presented by two fathers)*

Minister: The eyes of all wait upon you, O Lord,

Congregation: *And you give them their food in due season.*

Fathers: We present to God bread, the staff of life, as a token of our gratitude for his sending all things that are needful both for our souls and our bodies

Minister: Let us pray for all those whose daily work provides our food and clothing; those who work on land and sea; and let us remember that we do not live by bread alone.

All: *Praise him for our harvest store,*
He hath filled the garner floor;
For his mercies aye endure,
Ever faithful, ever sure.

The Gift of Milk *(Presented by two mothers)*

Minister: You open your hand,

Congregation: *And fill all things living with plenteousness.*

Mothers: We present to God this milk as a token of our gratitude for his loving care and as a symbol of human kindness to be shown to children and to the sick.

Minister: Let us pray for all the homes and hospitals in our land, and for our Church as it ministers the milk of God's word, that we may all grow unto salvation.

All: *All things living he doth feed,*
His full hand supplies their need;
For his mercies aye endure,
Ever faithful, ever sure.

The Gift of Fruit and Vegetables *(Presented by three young people)*

Minister: He brought forth grass for the cattle,

Congregation: *And green herb for the service of men.*

Young
People: We offer God some of the fruits of the earth as a token of our gratitude and as a symbol of the future entrusted to us.

Minister: Let us pray for schools, youth organizations, colleges and universities, that young people may grow in the knowledge of our Savior, follow Christ the King, and enthrone him in their hearts for ever.

All: *And hath bid the fruitful field*
Crops of precious increase yield;
For his mercies aye endure,
Ever faithful, ever sure.

The Gift of Flowers *(Presented by four children)*

Minister: Consider the lilies of the field, how they grow;

Congregation: *Even Solomon in all his glory was not arrayed like one of these.*

Children: We present these flowers and say "thank you" for all the beautiful things in God's world.

Minister: Let us pray that the beauties of the earth may teach us the beauty of God's love and goodness, and that we may enable our children to grow up in love and understanding.

All: *Praise him that he made the sun*
Day by day its course to run;
For his mercies aye endure,
Ever faithful, ever sure.

The Gifts of Industry *(Presented by three industrial workers)*

Minister: Whatever your hand finds to do,

Congregation: *Do with all your might.*

132

Workers: We present these gifts to God as a token of our gratitude for all his wondrous gifts of strength and craft and skill.

Minister: Let us pray that in industry and in commerce there may be freedom from distrust, bitterness, and dispute. May we all seek what is just and equal, and may we all live together in unity and love.

All: *God with all-commanding might*
Filled the new-made world with light;
For his mercies aye endure,
Ever faithful, ever sure.

The Gift of Money *(Presented by two lay leaders of the congregation)*

Minister: Bear one another's burdens,

Congregation: *And so fulfill the law of Christ.*

Lay leaders: We present the offering of this congregation as a token of our possessions which are all a trust from God.

Minister: Let us pray that Christians everywhere may be known for their industry, their right use of leisure, their sacrificial giving, and their honest, kindly dealing with one another, as people striving to love God and their neighbor as themselves.

All: *Let us blaze his name abroad,*
For of gods he is the God;
For his mercies aye endure,
Ever faithful, ever sure.

The Gift of Bread and Wine *(Presented by two deacons)*

Minister: As often as you eat this bread, and drink this cup,

Congregation: *You proclaim the Lord's death until he comes.*

Deacons: We present this bread and this wine, that by participating in the sacrament we may feed on Christ by faith and with thanksgiving.

Minister: Let us pray that as the wheat scattered over the fields has been harvested into this one loaf, so the Church may be gathered together from the ends of the earth into Christ's kingdom, and that offering ourselves as a living sacrifice, we may be strengthened to go forth into the world to serve God faithfully.

> All: *And for richer food than this,*
> *Pledge of everlasting bliss;*
> *For his mercies aye endure;*
> *Ever faithful, ever sure.*
>
> *Glory to our bounteous King;*
> *Glory let creation sing;*
> *For his mercies aye endure;*
> *Ever faithful, ever sure.*
> *Amen.*

WORSHIP FOR TODAY
HYMN STANZAS BY JOHN MILTON*

•80 A Litany of Confession and Compassion at Harvest Time

Surrounded by the beauty of God's creation, let us thank God for all the joy and wonder that come to us through the appreciation of beauty and color. And let us pray for those who are blind or whose sight is fading.
Lord, in your mercy:
Hear our prayer.

All the flowers, fruit and vegetables grown in our gardens remind us of the thousands of people who have no gardens where they can grow things and few open spaces where their children can play. Let us pray for children who have never picked a flower from their own garden or who have never climbed a tree. Let us pray also for parents facing each day the frustration of living in high-rise apartment buildings or in filthy slums.
Lord, in your mercy:
Hear our prayer.

The abundance of our harvest reminds us that millions never have enough to eat. Let us ask God's forgiveness for our indifference to the needs of others and for our forgetting that much of the wealth of this country has been gained by exploiting others. Let us pray that as a nation and as individuals we may take seriously our responsibilities for those who are starving.
Lord, in your mercy:
Hear our prayer.

Today we thank God for the provision of our needs as families and individuals, but God is also concerned for us as a community. Let us pray for our common life and for those in positions of leadership and authority

here; let us pray for those who have recently moved here and for those who find it difficult to accept the changes taking place in our community.
Lord, in your mercy:
Hear our prayer.

The beauty of creation and the abundant provision for our physical needs remind us to give thanks to God, but millions in our land and across the seas do not know of God's love for them and have never responded to Christ's invitation, "Come unto me and I will give you rest." Let us pray for those who have never entrusted their lives to Christ. Let us pray for ourselves and for all the Missionary Societies as, together, we tell people of the Lord Jesus Christ and of his love for them.
Lord, in your mercy:
Hear our prayer.

Today we have remembered to thank God for his goodness to us, but this reminds us that often we forget to thank him, and that we just take God and his love for granted. Let us ask for God's forgiveness and pray that we may never be complacent about the good things which we enjoy and are called by God to share generously with others.
Lord, in your mercy:
Hear our prayer. Amen.

PETER MARKBY
–PRAYERS FOR TODAY'S CHURCH

•81 World Hunger

Our Lord Jesus Christ gave himself to those who recognized their need, their hunger, their poverty in and of themselves, and their dependence on God. These were the people most able to receive him and to welcome his message and his word. So today we say: Lord, make us hungry.

For your Word and for your Spirit,	*Lord, make us hungry.*
For the bread of life,	*Lord, make us hungry.*
For understanding and compassion,	*Lord, make us hungry.*
For freedom, justice and peace,	*Lord, make us hungry.*
For an equal sharing of your good gifts,	*Lord, make us hungry.*

Our Lord Jesus Christ said, "If you then, who are evil, know how to give good gifts to your children, how much more will your Father who is in heaven give good things to those who ask him!" So today we turn to the Father once again and say: Lord, fill us.

With your hope and strength,	*Lord, fill us.*

With your boundless love and self-giving,	*Lord, fill us.*
With the power of Christ's death and resurrection,	*Lord, fill us.*
With his sensitivity to the needs of others,	*Lord, fill us.*
With trust in your will to save us all,	*Lord, fill us.*

That all may know you to be their Father and Christ to be the one whom you have sent,
Lord, make us bread broken for others.

That the rights and needs of all may be recognized and provided for,
Lord, make us bread broken for others.

That all may be fed and none go hungry,
Lord, make us bread broken for others.

That all may have life and have it in all its fulness,
Lord, make us bread broken for others.

That we may give thanks to you not only with our lips but in our lives,
Lord, make us bread broken for others.

That your will may be done on earth as it is in heaven,
Lord, make us bread broken for others.

(Silence)

Our Father in heaven,
  hallowed be your Name,
  your kingdom come,
  your will be done,
    on earth as in heaven.
Give us today our daily bread.
Forgive us our sins
  as we forgive those
    who sin against us.
Save us from the time of trial,
  and deliver us from evil.
For the kingdom, the power,
  and the glory are yours,
  now and for ever. Amen.

BREAD FOR THE WORLD

✝✝✝Prayer and ✝✝✝Society

The Nation

•82 For the Nation

(This litany is designed to be used on days of national celebration, or in times of national crisis.)

Mighty God: the earth is yours and the nations are your people. Take away our pride and bring to mind your goodness, so that, living together in this land, we may enjoy your gifts and be thankful.
Amen.

For clouded mountains, fields and woodland; for shoreline and running streams;
for all that makes our nation good and lovely;
We thank you, God.

For farms and villages where food is gathered to feed our people;
We thank you, God.

For cities where people talk and work together in factories, shops, or schools to shape those things we need for living;
We thank you, God.

For explorers, planners, statesmen; for prophets who speak out, and for silent faithful people; for all who love our land and guard our freedom;
We thank you, God.

For vision to see your purpose hidden in our nation's history, and courage to seek it in love given and received;
We thank you, God.

O God: your justice is like rock, and your mercy like pure flowing water. Judge and forgive us. If we have turned from you, return us to your way; for without you we are lost people.
Amen.

From brassy patriotism and a blind trust in power;
Deliver us, O God.

From public deceptions that weaken trust; from self-seeking in high political places;
Deliver us, O God.

From divisions among us of class or race; from wealth that will not share, and poverty that feeds on the food of bitterness;
Deliver us, O God.

From neglecting rights; from overlooking the hurt, the imprisoned, and the needy among us;
Deliver us, O God.

From a lack of concern for other lands and peoples; from narrowness of national purpose; from failure to welcome the peace you promise on earth;
Deliver us, O God.

Eternal God: before you nations rise and fall; they grow strong or wither by your design. Help us to repent of our country's wrong, an to choose your right in reunion and renewal.
Amen.

Give us a glimpse of the Holy City you are bringing to earth, where death and pain and crying will be gone away, and nations will gather in the light of your presence.
Great God, renew this nation.

Teach us peace, so that we may plow up battlefields and pound weapons into building tools, and learn to talk across old boundaries as brothers and sisters in your love.
Great God, renew this nation.

Talk sense to us, so that we may wisely end all prejudice, and may put a stop to cruelty, which divides or wounds the human family.
Great God, renew this nation.

Draw us together as one people who do your will, so that our land may be a light to nations, leading the way to your promised kingdom which is coming among us.
Great God, renew this nation.

Great God, eternal Lord: long years ago you gave our ancestors this land as a home for the free. Show us there is no law or liberty apart from you; and let us serve you modestly, as devoted people; through Jesus Christ our Lord.
Amen.

THE WORSHIPBOOK

•83 In Thanksgiving for Our Country

O eternal God, ruler of all the earth, we bless you for our country.
Bountifully have you given to us, beyond all our deserving. You have made
us heirs of what the untold ages have created: the majesty of upthrust
mountains, the green of wooded hills, the prairies rolling to their far
horizons, the fertile valleys where the rivers run. All that we can accomplish
rests on this which you have freely given. Hear us as we bring you the
tribute of our grateful hearts.

For all the mighty width of land from bordering sea to sea,
We thank you, O Lord.

For endless fields where the grain harvests ripen, for orchards with their
golden fruit,
We thank you, O Lord.

For cattle in the meadows, for wild life in the woods, for the fish in the
ocean and lakes and mountain streams, for the homely creatures of the farm,
and for the infinite beauty of winged birds,
We thank you, O Lord.

For rich ores hidden in the hills, for coal and oil and iron, and for all the
treasures of unnumbered mines,
We thank you, O Lord.

For the strength and skill of all the toiling multitude on whom our life
depends: on farms, in fishing fleets, in factories, and before the fires of
furnaces and mills,
We thank you, O Lord.

For the genius of inventors, for the imagination of engineers, for the daring
of those who have dreamed a mightier civilization and have fashioned their
dreams in stone and steel,
We thank you, O Lord.

For those who laid the railroads and launched the ships, for those who have
built the bridges and lifted the towers of cities to the sky,
We thank you, O Lord.

For all the host of men and women who in industry, in commerce, and in
communications hold the world together because they are dependable at their
daily posts,
We thank you, O Lord.

For all the servants of the mind, for scholars and teachers, for authors and
artists, and for all poets in word or deed who reveal the wideness and
wonder of the world,
We thank you, O Lord.

Yet we remember that as we have greatly received, so in the same measure
we are responsible. Forbid that we should betray our trust, or that the fire

which has been passed on to us should perish. Help us to be worthy of our forebears, and of their God.

To all the high desires of the pioneers and prophets,
O God, help us to be faithful.

To their belief in the possibilties of the common people,
O God, help us to be faithful.

To their passion for freedom and their readiness to live and die in its defense,
O God, help us to be faithful.

To their scorn of tyranny, and their trust in ordinary folk to rule themselves,
O God, help us to be faithful.

To their vision of a human commonwealth in which people from many lands might share,
O God, help us to be faithful.

To their their release from the prejudices and passions of an old world and their will to build a new,
O God, help us to be faithful.

O God, our mothers and fathers trusted in you
And were not confounded.

They lifted their faces to you
And were not ashamed.

So enlighten us, O Father, and lead us on your redeeming way; through Jesus Christ our Lord. *Amen.*

WALTER RUSSELL BOWIE

•84 Our National Life

Almighty God, giver of all good things:
We thank you for the natural majesty and beauty of this land.
They restore us, though we often destroy them
Heal us.

We thank you for the great resources of this nation. They make us rich, though we often exploit them.
Forgive us.

We thank you for the men and women who have made this country strong.
They are models for us, though we often fall short of them.
Inspire us.

We thank you for the torch of liberty which has been lit in this land. It has drawn people from every nation, though we have often hidden from its light. *Enlighten us.*

We thank you for the faith we have inherited in all its rich variety. It sustains our life, though we have been faithless again and again. *Renew us.*

Help us, O Lord, to finish the good work here begun. Strengthen our efforts to blot out ignorance and prejudice, and to abolish poverty and crime. And hasten the day when all our people, with many voices in one united chorus, will glorify your holy Name. *Amen.*

O judge of the nations, we remember before you with with grateful hearts the men and women of our country who in the day of decision ventured much for the liberties we now enjoy. Grant that we may not rest until all the people of this land share the benefits of true freedom and gladly accept its disciplines. This we ask in the Name of Jesus Christ our Lord. *Amen.*

THE BOOK OF COMMON PRAYER 1979

•85 A Litany of Thanksgiving for All Who Fought Peacefully for Freedom

O God, the Ruler of the nations, we thank you for men and women in our nation's past who fought, bravely and without shedding blood, for many kinds of freedom.
They knew that freedom is indivisible, and that freedom for some demands freedom for all.

We thank you for John Woolman and his fellow Quakers,
Who freed their slaves without approval from anyone except you;

For Harriet Beecher Stowe who, by kindling compassion for "Uncle Tom", set a nation's conscience on edge;
And for Martin Luther King who gave his life for the dream of "Black and White together".

We praise you, Father, for forgotten loners who strove to secure the first rights for workers;
And for great leaders of labor who were able to build upon their vision and their sacrifices.

We give you thanks, Father, for Horace Mann who fought to insure a basic education for every child, regardless of caste or class;
And for John Dewey who saw children not as computers to be programmed but as young persons to be helped to grow.

We praise you, O God, for the pioneers in the struggle for the liberation of women – for Susan B. Anthony, Elizabeth Cady Stanton, and others;
And for the single-minded devotion of many who spent themselves working for the day when every child would be a wanted child.

We praise you, O God, for Christians who loved you enough to realize that others might love you in a different way but love you just as well;
For Roger Williams who struck the first peaceful blow for religious freedom, and William Penn who created a commonwealth where all people could dwell in peace.

We thank you for missionaries who chose to live among Indians, slaves, or alien immigrants, because they wanted to bring them into the mainstream of our society;
And for John R. Mott and others who worked for unity, dramatizing the scandal of our divisions and the enlargement of Christian witness and service which reunion would bring.

For all these peaceful fighters for freedom in our nation's past, we thank you, O Lord;
And we pray that we may take our place alongside them in today's struggles for freedom, justice, and mercy; in the name of Jesus Christ who has set us all free. Amen.

JOHN R. BODO
–MODELS FOR MINISTERS I*

•86 The Fourth of July

O God, on this day of national celebration, help us to recall what brought this nation into being:
not human animosity but social dissatisfaction.
Our forebears sought the right to open up this broad land for the benefit of all who tilled its soil and tended its forests and developed its trade.
May we, their children,
examine our present reasons for existing as a nation.

"We hold these truths to be self-evident; that all men are created equal; that they are endowed by their creator with certain unalienable rights . . ."
Help us, O God, to respect this cherished conviction, so dear to ourselves, and to embody it in all our dealings with others.

"That among these rights are Life, Liberty and the Pursuit of Happiness."
Save us, O God, from wasting Life,
from turning Liberty into license,
and from pursuing goals that bring no Happiness
either to ourselves or to others.

"That to secure these rights, governments are instituted among men, deriving their just powers from the consent of the governed."
Give us, O God, a lively interest in the government of our land.
Let us consent to nothing that tramples on human dignity,
and save us from imposing upon government tasks that it cannot perform.
To this end make us self-governing and self-disciplined,
lest by default we invite tyranny and repression.

"That whenever any form of government becomes destructive of these ends, it is the right of the people to alter or to abolish it, and to institute new government, laying its foundation on such principles and organizing its powers in such form as to them shall seem most likely to effect their safety and happiness."
We pray, O God, for our President,
and for all entrusted with political power.
Strengthen them to take the risks of enlightened leadership.
And help us to conserve what is tried and tested and true;
to carry through what has been rightly begun;
and to amend what no longer promotes the common weal.
All this we pray through Jesus Christ our Lord. Amen.

THEODORE A. GILL
–MODELS FOR MINISTERS I*

•87 ...With Liberty and Justice for All

"And a foreigner you shall not oppress, for you know the heart of the foreigner, seeing that you yourselves were foreigners in the land of Egypt."
Next year let us celebrate in a world where everyone is free.

As we celebrate this year there are millions of poor in our own country; we will not be free until all these are free.
Next year let us celebrate in a world where everyone is free.

This year there are many thousands of migrant workers who are exploited to our selfish advantage and gain.
Next year let us celebrate in a world where everyone is free.

This year we celebrate in a world that fears destruction; we cannot be free until fear is ended.
Next year let us celebrate in a world where everyone is free.

This year we celebrate in a climate of oppression where people lack basic freedoms in [_____] and many other parts of the world.
Next year let us celebrate in a world where everyone is free.

We will not be free until all are free.
Next year let us celebrate in a world where everyone indeed is free. Amen.

LITURGY MAGAZINE*

•88 Thanksgiving Day

Let us give thanks to God our Father for all God's gifts so freely bestowed upon us.

For the beauty and wonder of your creation, in earth and sky and sea,
We thank you, Lord.

For all that is gracious in the lives of men and women, revealing the image of Christ,
We thank you, Lord.

For our daily food and drink, our homes and families, and our friends,
We thank you, Lord.

For minds to think, and hearts to love, and hands to serve,
We thank you, Lord.

For health and strength to work, and leisure to rest and play,
We thank you, Lord.

For the brave and courageous, who are patient in suffering and faithful in adversity,
We thank you, Lord.

For all valiant seekers after truth, liberty, and justice,
We thank you, Lord.

For the communion of saints, in all times and places,
We thank you, Lord.

Above all, we give you thanks for the great mercies and promises given to us in Christ Jesus our Lord;
To him be praise and glory, with you, O Father, and the Holy Spirit, now and for ever. Amen.

THE BOOK OF COMMON PRAYER 1979

•89 So Much to Be Thankful For

Presiding Minister:
As consumers, we are conditioned by our economy never to be satisfied. But God is a fantastic supplier, and so we stop and take a sample inventory on this special day for giving thanks.

Leader:
For the smell of new rain, for pumpkins, and Snoopy, for the aroma of homemade bread, for cotton candy, for funny-looking animals like giraffes and koalas and human beings; for these and all your gifts,
>*People: We give you thanks, good Lord.*

For the smell of fall in the air, for pay checks, and smoked ribs, for the intricate designs of window frost, and for ice cubes and ice cream; for these and all your gifts,
>*We give you thanks, good Lord.*

For clean sheets, and peanut butter, and perma-press, and stereo headphones, for vacations and seat belts, for escalators, and for views from tall buildings; for these and all your gifts,
>*We give you thanks, good Lord.*

For first romances and second romances, for eyes to see colors and ears to hear music and feet to dance, for dissenters and the right to dissent, for black and red and brown power, for pine trees and daisies, for newspapers and sandals and frogs; for these and all your gifts,
>*We give you thanks, good Lord.*

For parks and woodsmoke and snow, for the smell of leather, for funny buttons and powerful posters, for pecan pies and french fries, for re-cycling centers, for jet planes and parking spaces, for zoos and fountains and rock music and Bach music; for these and all your gifts,
>*We give you thanks, good Lord.*

(Silence)

Presiding Minister:
God, you overwhelm us with your goodness. And we have yet to mention your greatest gift of all, our brother Jesus! For these and all your gracious gifts, help us to learn how to live thankfully each day. *Amen.*

PRAYERS OF THE FAITHFUL

•90 Prayers for a National Holiday

Heavenly Father, we give you thanks for the wonder of creation, for the gifts of human life and for the blessing of human fellowship.
We thank you, Lord.

For Christ, your living Word, through whom we are taught the perfect way of life and the dignity of service,
We thank you Lord.

For your Spirit, who offers his gifts to us for the common good,
We thank you Lord.

For the blessing of community in our nation, and for those who have used your gifts to strengthen and enrich its life,
We thank you Lord.

For our President, and for all who serve as leaders in this land,
We thank you Lord.

Grant them, we pray, a vision of your will for your people; wisdom to fulfill their vocation of leadership in a nation of many races; strength and courage to carry out the duties of their calling; and the assurance of your presence, your power, and your love.
Lord, in your mercy
Hear our prayer.

We pray for all who are called to serve in times and places of crisis, in the face of racial and social tensions;
Lord, in your mercy
Hear our prayer.

In the Church's ministry of the Gospel, we ask for a clear message of your love and power;
Lord, in your mercy
Hear our prayer.

In federal, state and local government, for insight, integrity and courage;
Lord, in your mercy
Hear our prayer.

In the administration of law and in the defense of our people, for justice and humility, fairness and compassion;
Lord, in your mercy
Hear our prayer.

In industry and commerce, in trade and business, for mutual care and cooperation and a concern for the good of all;
Lord, in your mercy
Hear our prayer.

In art and music, theater and entertainment, sport and leisure, for
recognition that all gifts come from you to give to one another;
Lord, in your mercy
Hear our prayer.

In every mode of communication, in literature and press, radio and
television, for a vision of social good and for service to the truth;
Lord, in your mercy
Hear our prayer.

In education, in family and school and college, for a concern not only
with information but also with maturity and fulfillment of life;
Lord, in your mercy
Hear our prayer.

And finally, in the service of those in need and sickness, anxiety and
suffering, for a community that cares;
Lord, in your mercy
Hear our prayer.
Amen.

ADAPTED FROM THE SERVICE FOR THE SILVER JUBILEE OF QUEEN
ELIZABETH II*

Confession of Social Ills

•91 For the Isolated and the Alienated

My brothers and sisters,
so many men and women
waste away and get shriveled up
in a universe reduced to fit their limited vision.
Let us ask the Spirit of the Lord
to open up their hearts
to a greater and stronger love.
Lord, source of all love,
make us burn with charity.

For families turned in on themselves,
exclusive in their affections,
indifferent to the external world,
that they may notice
the needs and joys which surround them,
let us pray to the Lord.
Lord, source of all love,
make us burn with charity.

For troubled towns
where teenagers rebel
and no longer hope in adults;
for slum nieghborhoods
where, with no assistance from the rest of society,
the poor and alienated are dying,
let us pray to the Lord.
Lord, source of all love,
make us burn with charity.

For antagonistic groups, classes, races,
who see their own vengeance and their own security
in absolute, unbending terms;
for politicians
and national and international diplomats,
so that their concern for the common good
may go beyond defense
of the narrow interests of their constituents,
let us pray to the Lord.
Lord, source of all love,
make us burn with charity.

For Christian communities,
entrenched in their dogmas and practices,
that they may guard against seeing an enemy
in someone who disagrees,
a sinner in the unbeliever;
for the most uncompromising among us
in whose eyes every dialogue is already a compromise,
and adaptation to another's viewpoint means
abandoning the truth,
let us pray to the Lord.
Lord, source of all love,
make us burn with charity.

For all of us gathered at the Eucharist,
that throughout the entire world
those who today partake of the same bread
and the same communion cup
may become witnesses of the Lord
who made himself all things for all people;
and that each of us may willingly give our life and time
for the happiness of others,
let us pray to the Lord.
Lord, source of all love,
make us burn with charity.
Amen.

PRAYERS IN COMMUNITY

•92 For the Elderly

We remember before you, O Lord, with gratitude, with shame, and with
renewed concern, the many millions of older people in this country. We
pray for them, and especially for the elderly in this community.

(Silence)

The wisdom and experience that they have acquired in so many ways over so many years;
This we remember with gratitude.

The time they devote to loving and spoiling and listening to the young;
This we remember with gratitude.

Their adaptability to changing circumstances in a time when nothing seems to be permanenat or dependable;
This we remember with gratitude.

Their appreciation for nature, their love of travel, their curiosity and zest for life;
This we remember with gratitude.

Their courage in facing physical disability, suffering, and the approach of death;
This we remember with gratitude.

(Silence)

Our ignorning of their opinions and of their contributions so that they feel useless and unwanted;
This we remember with shame.

Our confining of them, the old with the old, in nursing homes and institutions;
This we remember with shame.

Our letting them live on shrinking incomes and on inadequate food;
This we remember with shame.

Our failure to design or adapt our churches so that they may enter and move about in them with ease;
This we remember with shame.

Our letting them die slow and desperate deaths in unheated, unvisited apartments;
This we remember with shame.

(Silence)

Almighty God, help us with renewed concern to celebrate and use the vast treasure of wisdom, knowledge and experience that comes with the living out of many years.

Quicken us with compassion that we may make this community and this nation a place where people of every age, however old, however weak, may be accorded all the justice, all the dignity, and all the worth that is theirs by right as children of your one family on earh; through Jesus Christ our Lord. Amen.

JEFFERY W. ROWTHORN

•93 A Lament for Creation

And God said, "Let there be light," and there was light. And God saw that the light was good and God called the light Day.

And we said, "Let there be darkness." For we loved the darkness more than the light.

And there was darkness.

And we called the darkness reality, but the light we called naivete. And we saw that our darkness was evil.

And God said, "Let there be a firmament in the midst of the waters." And it was so. And God called the firmament Heaven.

And we said, "Let the firmament be filled with Strontium 90 and guided missiles, with smoke and gasses and industrial waste."

And we called the firmament our predicament, and some called it Hell.

And we looked at all we had done, and it was evil.

And God said, "Let there be lights in the firmament of the heavens". . . and God set them in the firmament to rule over day and night. And God saw that it was good.

And we said, "Let us build our own satellites to watch over each other with electronic eyes and listen to each other with electronic ears."

And it was so.

And we saw that it was evil.

And God said, "Let the waters bring forth swarms of living creatures, and let the birds fly above the earth." And God gave the swarming things to us.

And we said, "Let us spray all the swarming things, let us spray them with DDT. Let us dump refuse into the waters, and explode our atomic weapons below the sea."

And it was so.

And we looked at all we had done, and it was evil.

And God said, "Let the earth bring forth living creatures according to their kinds, cattle and creeping things and beasts of the earth according to their kinds.

And we said, "Let us slaughter the cattle which roam the fields, the beasts which lurk in the jungle, and the creeping things in the forest."

And it was so.

And we saw what we had done, and it was evil.

And God said, "Let us make men and women in our image, after our likeness, and give them dominion over many things."

And we said, "Let us make God in our image, after our likeness, and let God have dominion over few things. Then we shall have someone to support our prejudices, to approve our wars, to blame for our failures."

And it was so.

And we saw everything we had made, and behold, it was very evil.

And there was evening and there was morning, a last day.

(Silence)

Lord, have mercy

Christ, have mercy.

Lord, have mercy.
Amen.

UNION THEOLOGICAL SEMINARY

•94 For Deliverance

Lord, save your world; in bitter need
To you your children raise their plea;
We wait your liberating deed
To signal hope and set us free.

Brothers and Sisters, let us confess our corporate and individual failings before the Lord.

(Silence)

We have heard the call to reconciliation, yet we are still divided, even within the Church.
Lord, have mercy

We have been shown the peace that passes understanding, but we are still at war, within ourselves, and with each other.
Lord, have mercy.

Lord, save your world; our souls are bound
In iron chains of fear and pride;
High walls of ignorance abound
And faces from each other hide.

We have been given dominion over all the earth, yet we still clamor for power over our neighbors.
Christ, have mercy.

We have been led into the light, but we have returned to the darkness.
Christ, have mercy.

Lord, save your world; we strive in vain
To save ourselves without your aid;
What skill and science slowly gain
Is soon to evil ends betrayed.

We have seen God revealed in the flesh, yet we still cling to our doubts.
Lord, have mercy.

We have seen our Lord Jesus Christ suffering for us, but we prefer lives of comfort which avoid strife and sacrifice.
Lord, have mercy.

Lord, save your world, since you have sent
The Savior whom we sorely need;
For us his tears and blood were spent
That from our bonds we might be freed.

(Silence)

We confess these and all our other sins and errors for which we ourselves are responsible. We are humbled, and we come asking forgiveness.

Brothers and Sisters, believe the good news of the Gospel:
In Jesus Christ we are forgiven. Thanks be to God.

Then save us now, by Jesus' power,
And use the lives your love sets free
To bring at last the glorious hour
When all shall find your liberty.
Amen.

UNION THEOLOGICAL SEMINARY
HYMN STANZAS BY ALBERT F. BAYLY*

•95 A Twentieth-Century Litany for Deliverance

Leader 1:	From the accidents of our history,
Leader 2:	And from the ironies of our history;
All:	*Good Lord, deliver us.*

Leader 1:	From universal education leaving millions unenlightentd,
Leader 2:	And from the enlightened betrayed in the maze of their own ingenuities;
All:	*Good Lord, deliver us.*

Leader 1:	From the capitalist destruction of the capitalist ethic,
Leader 2:	And from the socialist rejection of the socialist vision;
All:	*Good Lord, deliver us.*

Leader 1:	From specialists without spirit, and sensualists without heart,
Leader 2:	And from technology become tyranny, and revolution become oppression;
All:	*Good Lord, deliver us.*

Leader 1:	From long lives ending in slow deterioration,
Leader 2:	And good lives ending in sudden assassination;
All:	*Good Lord, deliver us.*

Leader 1:	From Protestants who no longer say, "Here I stand",
Leader 2:	And from Catholics who no longer cry, "Behold, the Lamb of God",
Leader 1:	And from churches which no longer preach, "Jesus Christ as Lord, and ourselves as your servants for Jesus' sake";
All:	*Good Lord, deliver us.*
	Good Lord, deliver us.

Leader 2:	Through the accidents and ironies of our history,
All:	*Good Lord, deliver us.*

Leader 1:	Through the short reigns of wise and generous Popes,
Leader 2:	And the long trauma of Vietnam and Watergate;
All:	*Good Lord, deliver us.*

Leader 1:	Through human suffering bringing Christians and Marxists into dialogue,
Leader 2:	And economic pressures bringing workers and employers out of deadlock;
All:	*Good Lord, deliver us.*

Leader 1:	Through fuel shortages requiring us to take other nations seriously,
Leader 2:	And lower speed limits enabling us to take other lives seriously;
All:	*Good Lord, deliver us.*

Leader 1:	Through earthrise seen in awe from the moon,
Leader 2:	And mushroom clouds seen in awe on the screen;
All:	*Good Lord, deliver us.*

Leader 1:	Through finding ourselves called to ministry,
Leader 2:	And finding others ready to minister to us,
Leader 1:	And finding churches ready to change and to die as the price of ministry;
All:	*Good Lord, deliver us.*
	Good Lord, deliver us.

Leader 2:	From subsisting with necessity to living with freedom,
Leader 1:	From the claustrophobia of abundance to the opportunities of shortage;
All:	*Good Lord, deliver us.*

Leader 2:	From human determinism to divine initiative,
Leader 1:	From the Remembrance of Things Past to the City of God
All:	*Good Lord, deliver us.*

In the best of times and the worst of times,
In the age of wisdom and the age of foolishness,
In the season of light and the season of darkness,
In the spring our our hope and the winter of our despair,
Good Lord, deliver us.
Amen.

JEFFERY W. ROWTHORN

•96 Confession of a Split Personality

We build nuclear bombs to destroy the world,
And we use nuclear power to lighten the darkness.

We have brought many nations together under one roof,
And we have used the United Nations to our own advantage.

We fly faster than the sun,
And we crawl in traffic jams.

We have died in Vietnam,
And we have walked on the moon.

(Silence)

O Come, O Come, Emmanuel
And ransom captive Israel
That mourns in lonely exile here
Until the Son of God appear.

We have beaten people with clubs,
And we have built courtrooms to keep them free.

We care about our brothers and sisters in the ghettos,
And we live in opulent comfort.

We litter the land with garbage,
And we work to conserve its beauty.

We have built schools to educate the young,
And we have made them battlefields for prejudice.

(Silence)

O Come, O Come, Emmanuel
And ransom captive Israel
That mourns in lonely exile here
Until the Son of God appear.

We are rightly proud,
And we are rightly ashamed.

We are able to do all things,
And yet the will to do them is lacking.

In our minds we are God's willing servants, but in our own nature we are
bound fast to the law of sin and death.
Who on earth can set us free from the agony of this condition?

(Silence)

O Come, O Come, Emmanuel
And ransom captive Israel
That mourns in lonely exile here
Until the Son of God appear.
Amen.

JEFFERY W. ROWTHORN*

•97 A Litany of Modern Ills

From hunger and unemployment, and from enforced eviction:
Good Lord, deliver us.

From unjust sentences and unjust wars:
Good Lord, deliver us.

From neglect by parents, neglect by children, and neglect by callous institutions:
Good Lord, deliver us.

From cancer and stroke, ulcers, madness, and senility:
Good Lord, deliver us.

From famine and epidemic, from overcrowding of the planet, and from pollution of the soil, the air, and the waters:
Good Lord, deliver us.

From segregation and prejudice, from harassment, discrimination, and brutality:
Good Lord, deliver us.

From the concentration of power in the hands of ignorant, threatened, or hasty leaders:
Good Lord, deliver us.

From propaganda, fads, frivolity, and untruthfulness:
Good Lord, deliver us.

From arrogance, narrowness and meanness, from stupidity and pretence:
Good Lord, deliver us.

From boredom, apathy, and fatigue, from lack of conviction, from fear, self-satisfaction, and timidity:
Good Lord, deliver us.

From retribution at the hands of our victims, and from the consequences of our own folly:
Good Lord, deliver us.

From resignation and despair, from cynicism and manipulation:
Good Lord, deliver us.

Through all unmerited suffering, our own and that of others:
Good Lord, deliver us.

Through the unending cry of all peoples for justice and freedom:
Good Lord, deliver us.

Through all concern and wonder, love and creativity:

Good Lord, deliver us.

In our strength and our weakness, in occasional success and eventual failure:
Good Lord, deliver us.

In aloneness and community, in the days of action and the time of our dying:
Good Lord, deliver us.

By the needs of humanity and of the earth, and not by our own merits or deserving:
Good Lord, deliver us.

Deliver us, Good Lord, by opening our eyes and unstopping our ears, that we may hear your word and do your will:
Good Lord, deliver us. Amen.

THE COVENANT OF PEACE
–A LIBERATION PRAYER BOOK

•98 A Confession of Wrong in Our Society

All: *Almighty and most merciful Father, we have erred and strayed from thy ways like lost sheep.*

First
voice: We have strayed from our own responsibilities to families and communities, thinking that we would thus be free.

All: *We have followed too much the devices and desires of our own hearts.*

Second
voice: We have been too sentimental and at the same time have followed too much the logic of our minds; we have built great universities to search out truth, then hidden behind their ivied walls to protect ourselves from strife and danger.

All: *We have offended against thy holy laws.*

First
voice: We have allowed our communities and nations to respect selfishness and injustice and have washed our hands of the "due process of law."

All: *We have left undone those things which we ought to have done.*

Second
voice: We have been irresponsible in our economic life and allowed
unrighteousness to hold sway in politics and the struggle for
power.
All: *And we have done those things which we ought not to have
done.*

First
voice: We have lived at the expense of our poorer brothers and
sisters at home and abroad; we have used the terrible
destructiveness of science against our enemies.
All: *And there is no health in us.*

Second
voice: There is conflict in the depths of our souls which has driven
us into sickness of mind and body.
All: *But thou, O Lord, have mercy upon us, miserable offenders,*

First
voice: Who have considered ourselves untainted by the evils of our
modern world.
All: *Spare thou those, O God, who confess their faults,*

Second
voice: Be they personal, social, cultural or religious sins.
All: *Restore thou those who are penitent*

First
voice: And would change both themselves and their society,
All: *According to thy promises declared unto mankind in Christ
Jesus our Lord,*

Second
voice: Through whom together we are raised up into thy kingdom
on earth and in heaven.
All: *And grant, O most merciful Father, for his sake, that we may
hereafter live a godly, righteous and sober life*

First
voice: Ordered by thy law and freed by thy grace.
All: *To the glory of thy holy name. Amen.*

THE STUDENT PRAYER BOOK
–AND THE BOOK OF COMMON PRAYER 1928*

•99 A Confession of Social Failure

The confusion of morals
O Lord, forgive.

The breakdown of social restraints
O Lord, forgive.

The increase of crime and violence
O Lord, forgive.

The commercialization of sex
O Lord, forgive.

The traffic in drugs
O Lord, forgive.

The exploitation of teenagers
O Lord, forgive.

The apathy and disenchantment of young people
O Lord, forgive.

Our loss of vision
O Lord, forgive.

Our moral cowardice
O Lord, forgive.

Our failure as parents and adults
O Lord, forgive.

Our self-seeking and self-indulgence
O Lord, forgive.

Our love of money and possessions
O Lord, forgive.

Our connivance at dishonesty and corruption
O Lord, forgive.

Our unwillingness to serve and give of ourselves
O Lord, forgive.

Almighty God, have mercy on you (us), forgive you (us) all your (our) sins through our Lord Jesus Christ, strengthen you (us) in all goodness, and by the power of the Holy Spirit keep you (us) in eternal life. *Amen.*

THE ANGLICAN CATHEDRAL, LIVERPOOL
–PRAYERS FOR TODAY'S CHURCH

•100 Litany of Social Penitence

O God, our Father, who hast made us thy human children as one family in thee, so that what concerns any must concern all, we confess the evils we have done and the good we have left undone. We have spent our strength too often upon the tower of Babel of our own pride, and have forgotten the city that hath foundations, whose builder and maker is God. We have been content that we ourselves should prosper though many might be poor, that a few should feast while multitudes were famished both in body and in soul. O thou who hast taught us that whatsoever we sow, that shall we also reap, help us to repent before thy judgement comes.

(Silence)

For the clouded eyes that see no further than our own advantage,
We confess our sin, O Lord.

For the dulled imagination that does not know what others suffer,
We confess our sin, O Lord.

For the willingness to profit by injustice which we have not striven to prevent,
We confess our sin, O Lord.

For the selfishness that is quick to gain and slow to give,
We confess our sin, O Lord.

For the unconcern that makes us cry, Am I my brother's keeper?
We confess our sin, O Lord.

O thou who art ever merciful, take away the evil of our conscious and unconscious wrongs, forgive us for our unfaithfulness to the vision of thy kingdom, and grant to us a better purpose for the days to come.

From acquiescence in old iniquities,
Save us, O Lord.

From indifference to the human cost of anything we covet,
Save us, O Lord.

From the greed that wastes the resources of this rich earth,
Save us, O Lord.

From the ignorance that wastes the lives of men and women through unemployment, poverty and deprivation,
Save us, O Lord.

From the cruelty that exploits the needy and defenseless,
Save us, O Lord.

From the blasphemy against the Spirit that sells the bodies and souls of children to the golden idol of success,
Save us, O Lord.

From false leadership in business and in government, and above all from feebleness in the people that lets false leaders rise to power,
Save us, O Lord.

Unless the Lord build the house,
Their labor is but vain that build it.

Unless the Lord keep the city,
The watchman waketh but in vain.

But he that sitteth upon the throne said,
Behold, I make all things new.

Even so, O God, let thy redemptive purposes work through us to build a new and better order on this earth, for the blessing of thy people and the glory of thy name; through Jesus Christ our Lord. *Amen.*

WALTER RUSSELL BOWIE

• 101 "As You Did It to One of the Least of These My Brethren, You Did It to Me"

O God, who is old, and lives on fifty dollars a month, in one crummy room and can't get outside,
Help us to see you.

O God, who is fifteen and in the sixth grade,
Help us to see you.

O God, who is three and whose belly aches in hunger,
Help us to see you, as you have seen us in Jesus Christ our Lord.

O God, who sleeps in a bed with your four brothers and sisters, and who cries and no one hears you,
Help us to touch you.

O God, who has no place to sleep tonight except an abandoned car, an alley or deserted building,
Help us to touch you.

O God, who is uneducated, unskilled, unwanted, and unemployed,
Help us to touch you, as you have touched us in Jesus Christ our Lord.

O God, who was laid off last week and can't pay the rent or feed the kids,
Help us to be with you.

O God, who is poor and on welfare and told you don't want to work,
Help us to be with you.

O God, who is dressed by the suburbs from the church clothing store,
Help us to be with you, as you are with us in Jesus Christ our Lord.

O God, who is chased by the cops, who sits in jail for seven months with no charges brought, waiting for the Grand Jury and no money for bail,
Help us to know you.

O God, who hangs on the street corners, who tastes the grace of cheap wine and the sting of the needle,
Help us to know you.

O God, who pays too much rent for a lousy apartment because you speak Spanish,
Help us to know you, as you know us in Jesus Christ our Lord.

O God, who is uprooted by Urban Renewal and removed from your neighborhood,
Help us to stand with you.

O God, whose church down the street closed and moved away,
Help us to stand with you.

O God, whose elected leaders only know you exist at election time and represent themselves and not the people,
Help us to stand with you, as you stand with us in Jesus Christ our Lord.

O God, who is poor and has all sorts of programs being planned for you,
Help us to join you.

O God, who is unorganized, and without strength to change your world, your city, your neighborhood,
Help us to join you.

O God, who is fed up with it all and who is determined to do something, who is organizing people for power to change the world,
Help us to join you, as you have joined us in Jesus Christ our Lord. Amen.

ROBERT W. CASTLE, JR.
–PRAYERS FROM THE BURNED-OUT CITY*

•102 For the Suburbs

O God, we have meant to love and serve you better than we do, but we have not. Our streets are lined with trees, our houses warm, our friends good, our children well-fed. We have meant to thank you with our lives, but we have not.
O God, forgive us and teach us your ways.

We have meant to listen for your voice, but we have been too busy to hear you very often. When we have heard you, we have meant to obey you, but we have forgotten – or at times we have been too afraid.
O God, forgive us and teach us your ways.

We have set up a comfortable family life as our highest goal and closed our eyes to the greater demands of your love. We have filled our lives with too many things to do and too many things to care for.
O God, forgive us and teach us your ways.

We have set ourselves apart from our poorer city neighbors and sometimes forget that they are even there. We try not to think of the hungry in other lands too often, because there are so many.
O God, forgive us and teach us your ways.

We have lived in anxiety lest our private world explode in pain and terror, and we have looked towards fear and away from you.
O God, forgive us and teach us to hope.

We have not dared to put our trust in you, but have put it in soldiers and armaments, and we are still afraid.
O God, forgive us and teach us to trust.

We have considered spending vast sums on weaponry to save us from destruction, but seldom spoken about spending vast sums to feed the poor and hungry.
O God, forgive us and teach us to love.

We have meant to serve you in everything we do, but we have given you only the leftover hour, the spare energy and the momentary prayer.
O God, forgive us and teach us your ways. Amen

AVERY BROOKE

Sickness and Healing

• 103 For Healing

God the Father, whose will for all is health and salvation;
Have mercy on us.

God the Son, who came that we might have life and have it more
abundantly;
Have mercy on us.

God the Spirit, whose temple our bodies are;
Have mercy on us.

Holy Trinity, in whom we live, and move, and have our being;
Have mercy on us.

Son of David, you healed all who came to you in faith;
Heal your people, Lord.

Son of Man, you sent forth your disciples to preach the Gospel and heal the
sick;
Heal your people, Lord.

Son of God, you pardon our sins and heal our infirmities;
Heal your people, Lord.

Eternal Christ, your abiding Spirit renews our minds;
Heal your people, Lord.

Lord Jesus, your holy Name is a medicine of healing and a pledge of eternal
life;
Heal your people, Lord.

We pray that you will hear us, O Lord; and that you will grant your grace to make the sick well;
Hear us, and make us whole.

That you will give patience, courage, and faith to all who are disabled by injury or sickness;
Hear us, and make us whole.

That you will give speedy healing, relief from pain, and fearless confidence to all sick children;
Hear us, and make us whole.

That you will grant your strengthening presence to all who are about to undergo an operation;
Hear us, and make us whole.

That you will sustain those who face long illness, bearing them up as on eagles' wings;
Hear us, and make us whole.

That you will comfort those who endure continual pain, pouring upon them the sweet balm of your Spirit;
Hear us, and make us whole.

That you will grant to all sufferers the refreshment of quiet sleep;
Hear us, and make us whole.

That you will abide with all who are lonely or despondent, having no one to comfort them;
Hear us, and make us whole.

That you will restore all who are in mental darkness to soundness of mind and cheerfulness of heart;
Hear us, and make us whole.

That by sickness endured and sickness observed you will teach us our mortality, that we may prepare for death with fortitude and meet it with hope;
Hear us, and make us whole.

That you will give your wisdom in ample measure to doctors and nurses, that with knowledge, skill, and patience, they may minister to the sick;
Hear us, and make us whole.

That you will guide by your good Spirit all who search for the causes of sickness and disease;
Hear us and make us whole.

Jesus, Lamb of God:
Have mercy on us.

Jesus, bearer of our sins:
Have mercy on us.

Jesus, redeemer of the world:
Give us your peace.

Our Father, who art in heaven,
hallowed be thy Name,
thy kingdom come,
thy will be done,
on earth as it is in heaven.
Give us this day our daily bread.
And forgive us our trespasses,
as we forgive those who trespass against us.
And lead us not into temptation,
but deliver us from evil.
For thine is the kingdom, and the power, and the glory,
for ever and ever. Amen.

Almighty God, giver of life and health: Your Son came into this ailing world to make your children whole. Send your blessing on all who are sick and on all who minister to them; that when they are restored to health of body and mind, they may give thanks to you in your Church; through the same Jesus Christ our Lord. *Amen.*

MORTON STONE
–PRAYERS, THANKSGIVINGS, LITANIES

•104 Christ the Healer

Jesus went on from there and reached the shores of the Sea of Galilee, and went up into the hills. He sat there, and large crowds came to him bringing the lame, the crippled, the blind, the dumb and many others; these they put down at his feet, and he cured them. The crowds were astonished to see the dumb speaking, the cripples whole again, the lame walking and the blind with their sight, and they praised the God of Israel. *(Matthew 15:29–31)*

Lord Jesus, Son of David and Son of God,
Heal and save us.

Lord Jesus, who bore our griefs and carried our sorrow,
Heal and save us.

Lord Jesus, who went about preaching the Good News and curing all kinds of disease and sickness,

Heal and save us.

Lord Jesus, who raised to life the daughter of Jairus, and the only son of the widow of Nain, and Lazarus whom you loved,
Heal and save us.

Lord Jesus, who cured Simon Peter's mother-in-law of a fever, and the woman suffering from hemorrhages,
Heal and save us.

Lord Jesus, who delivered the Gadarene demoniacs, and the tormented daughter of the Canaanite woman,
Heal and save us.

Lord Jesus, who cured the centurion's paralyzed servant, and the dumb epileptic boy,
Heal and save us.

Lord Jesus, who restored the sight of Bartimaeus, the blind beggar of Jericho, and who purified many lepers,
Heal and save us.

Lord Jesus, who cured the man with the withered hand, and who made cripples whole again,
Heal and save us.

Lord Jesus, who commanded your disciples to lay hands on the sick and to anoint them with oil to cure them,
Heal and save us.

Lord Jesus, who ordered your disciples to cast out demons in your name,
Heal and save us.

(Here the sick may be prayed for by name.)

Heavenly Father, giver of life and health: Comfort and relieve your sick servants, and give your power of healing to those who minister to their needs, that they may be strengthened in their weakness and have confidence in your loving care; through Jesus Christ our Lord. Amen.

PRAY LIKE THIS
AND THE BOOK OF COMMON PRAYER 1979

• 105 A Thanksgiving for Hospitals

O God, we give you thanks that there are such places as hospitals and infirmaries and nursing-homes, and we remember before you with gratitude and concern all who minister in them to the sick and the needy.

(Silence)

For places
where the ill and the weak and the old
are not looked on as a nuisance,
but where they find
loving care and attention,
We give you thanks, good Lord.

For doctors
who have the skill
to find out what is wrong
and to put it right again,
We give you thanks, good Lord.

For nurses
who throughout the day and night
attend to those in discomfort, distress and pain,
We give you thanks, good Lord.

For all the people
who do the many jobs which have to be done,
if the work of a hospital is to go on:
for technicians, dispensers and dieticians,
We give you thanks, good Lord.

For social workers, nurses' aides, and orderlies,
We give you thanks, good Lord.

For secretaries, typists and clerks,
We give you thanks, good Lord.

For porters and ambulance drivers,
cooks and kitchen maids,
We give you thanks, good Lord.

For hospital chaplains
who bring prayer and sacrament, hope and comfort,
to patients and staff alike,
We give you thanks, good Lord.

For all who visit the sick,
coming because they care and want to help,
We give you thanks, good Lord.

For pharmacologists and all who discover new drugs, new forms of
treatment, new ways to conquer old diseases,
We give you thanks, good Lord.

For health plans and for all who work to make healing fully and freely available to the sick,
We give you thanks, good Lord.

(Silence)

Almighty God, whose blessed Son Jesus Christ went about doing good, healing all manner of sickness and all manner of disease among the people: continue, we pray, that his gracious work among us, especially in the hospitals and nursing-homes of our community. Cheer, heal, and sanctify the sick. Grant to the physicians, surgeons, and nurses wisdom and skill, sympathy and patience; and assist with your blessing all who are seeking to prevent suffering and to forward your good purposes of love; through Jesus Christ our Lord. *Amen.*

WILIAM BARCLAY
–PRAYERS FOR HELP AND HEALING

•106 For Those in Distress

Lord Jesus, when you were on earth, they brought the sick to you and you healed them all. We ask you now to bless all those in sickness, in weakness, and in pain.

Those who are blind and who cannot see the light of the sun, the beauty of the world, or the faces of their friends;
Lighten their darkness, and give them hope.

Those who are deaf and who cannot hear the voices which speak to them;
Lighten their darkness, and give them hope.

Those who are helpless and who must lie in bed while others go out and in;
Lighten their darkness, and give them hope.

Those whose minds have lost their reason;
Lighten their darkness, and give them hope.

Those who are so nervous that they cannot cope with life;
Lighten their darkness, and give them hope.

Those who worry about everything;
Lighten their darkness, and give them hope.

Those who must face life with some disability;
Lighten their darkness, and give them hope.

Those whose weakness means that they must always be careful;

Lighten their darkness, and give them hope.

Those who are lame or handicapped and who cannot enter into any of the strenuous activities or pleasures of life;
Lighten their darkness, and give them hope.

Those who have been crippled by accident or illness;
Lighten their darkness, and give them hope.

Grant, Lord, that we, in our health and strength, may never find those who are weak or handicapped a nuisance; inspire us by your unfailing compassion to do and give all that we can to help them, and to make life easier for them. In Christ's name we pray. *Amen.*

WILLIAM BARCAY
–EPILOGUES AND PRAYERS

•107 For Those Whose Lives Are Difficult

O God, our Father, we pray for those whose life at this time is very difficult.

Those who have difficult decisions to make, and who honestly do not know what is the right thing to do;
Jesus said: "Come to me, all whose work is hard, whose load is heavy, and I will give you rest."

Those who have difficult tasks to do and to face, and who fear that they may fail in them;
Jesus said: "Come to me, all whose work is hard, whose load is heavy, and I will give you rest."

Those who have difficult temptations to face, and who know only too well that they may give in to them, if they try to meet them alone;
Jesus said: "Set your troubled hearts at rest; trust in God always, trust also in me."

Those who have a difficult time coping with life, and who are tempted to suicide;
Jesus said: "Set your troubled hearts at rest; trust in God always, trust also in me."

Those who have a difficult temperament and nature to master, and who know that they can be their own worst enemies;
Jesus said: "Father, if it be your will, take this cup from me; yet not my will but yours be done."

Those who have difficult people to work with, and who suffer unjust treatment, unfair criticism, unappreciated work;
Jesus said: "Father, if it be your will, take this cup from me; yet not my will but yours be done."

Lord, in the midst of our difficulties and among all the changes and chances of this mortal life, help us to remember that you do not faint or grow weary.
For those who wait for the Lord shall renew their strength,
they shall mount up with wings as eagles,
they shall run and not be weary,
they shall walk and not faint. Amen.

WILLIAM BARCLAY
–EPILOGUES AND PRAYERS

• 108 Prisoners and Prisons

We pray first for those who are responsible for the maintenance of law and order in our community; for those who administer justice in the courts; and for those who are the victims of crime, violence and deceit.
Lord, hear us.

We pray for all prisoners, especially for those who are facing long sentences, and those who have lost faith in themselves and others, and have little hope for the future.
Lord, hear us.

We pray for young people; for those who have already come up against the law in juvenile and family courts; for those on probation, and those who are being drawn into crime.
Lord, hear us.

We pray for parents, teachers, youth leaders and clergy, and for all who try to help the young escape from the sordid and the second-rate, and to find a true purpose in life.
Lord, hear us.

We pray for all those who have the custody and care of prisoners; for prison wardens, chaplains and officers; for the Justice Department, and those who shape and direct our correctional institutions.
Lord, hear us.

We pray for all those who have a special concern for the after-care of offenders: probation officers, wardens of halfway houses, and employers of former prisoners.

Lord, hear us.

We pray for those who have been released from prison; those who have managed to make good and those who continue to find the going hard; and we ask that we may learn to be as forgiving of others as we know God to be forgiving of us.
Lord, hear us.

We pray for ourselves as members of the community; and we ask that our right respect for law and order may not stifle our compassion and concern for those who have not lived up to the accepted standards of our society.
Lord, hear us.

Lord Jesus, for our sake you were condemned as a criminal: Visit our jails and prisons with your pity and judgement. Remember all prisoners, and bring the guilty to repentance and amendment of life according to your will, and give them hope for their future. When any are held unjustly, bring them release; forgive us, and teach us to improve our justice. Remember those who work in these institutions; keep them humane and compassionate; and save them from becoming brutal or callous. And since what we do for those in prison, O Lord, we do for you, constrain us to improve their lot. All this we ask for your mercy's sake. *Amen.*

PRAYERS FOR TODAY'S CHURCH
AND THE BOOK OF COMMON PRAYER 1979*

Death and Dying

• 109 For the Dying

(Also suitable for use on Good Friday evening)

God the Father,
have mercy on us.

God the Son,
have mercy on us.

God the Holy Spirit,
have mercy on us.

Holy, blessed, and glorious Trinity,
have mercy on us.

God, who took the form of a servant and shared the life of suffering and sorrow,
have mercy on us.

God, who bore our weaknesses and healed our sicknesses,
have mercy on us.

God, who became obedient unto death, even death on a cross,
have mercy on us.

God, who at the beginning breathed life into man, and appointed the hour of our death,
have mercy on us.

Hear our prayers, good Jesus, and grant that, dying to sin here, we may live for you in heaven:
Good Jesus, hear us.

May we, remaining your faithful soldiers and servants here, receive hereafter the crown of glory:
Good Jesus, hear us.

May we accept with patience all the pains of death, knowing that you have borne them all as one of us:
Good Jesus, hear us.

Be with us in the valley of the shadow of death:
Good Jesus, hear us.

Let us not, at our last hour, fall away from you:
Good Jesus, hear us.

Forgive us our sins, and strengthen us with the Bread of Life:
Good Jesus, hear us.

Let us die in your faith and fear, in sure and certain hope of the resurrection to eternal life:
Good Jesus, hear us.

Deliver us, Lord, at our last hour: as you delivered Enoch and Elijah from the death which must come to all,
So save and deliver us.

As you delivered Noah from the flood,
So save and deliver us.

As you delivered Job from his affliction,
So save and deliver us.

As you delivered Isaac from the knife,
So save and deliver us.

As you delivered Lot from Sodom,
So save and deliver us.

As you delivered the children of Israel from Pharoah,
So save and deliver us.

As you delivered Daniel from the lions' den,
So save and deliver us.

As you delivered the three young men from the fiery furnace,
So save and deliver us.

As you delivered Esther and her people from the power of Haman,
So save and deliver us.

As you delivered David from Saul and from Goliath,
So save and deliver us.

As you delivered Peter from prison and Paul from his enemies,
So save and deliver us.

As you have always delivered from evil those who put their trust in you,
So save and deliver us.

Deliver us, Lord on that fearful day, when the heavens and the earth shall pass away, when you shall come to judge the world by fire:
Save and deliver us.

In the day of judgement, when the books are opened, and the dead, great and small, shall stand before you:
Save and deliver us.

Holy God, holy and strong, holy and immortal:
Have mercy on us.

Jesus, Lamb of God:
Have mercy on us.

Jesus, bearer of our sins:
Have mercy on us.

Jesus, redeemer of the world:
Give us your peace.

Our Father, who art in heaven,
hallowed be thy Name,
thy kingdom come,
thy will be done,
on earth as it is in heaven.
Give us this day our daily bread.
And forgive us our trespasses,
as we forgive those who trespass against us.
And lead us not into temptation,
but deliver us from evil.
For thine is the kingdom, and the power, and the glory,
for ever and ever. Amen.

Happy are the dead who die in the faith of Christ.
Even so, says the Spirit, for they rest from their labors. Amen.

PRAYERS FOR USE AT THE ALTERNATIVE SERVICES

178

•110 A Commendation at the Time of Death

Depart, O Christian soul, out of this world;
Amen.

In the name of God the Father Almighty who created you.
Amen.

In the name of Jesus Christ who redeemed you.
Amen.

In the name of the Holy Spirit who sanctifies you.
Amen.

May your rest be this day in peace,
and your dwelling place in the Paradise of God.

Into your hands, O merciful Savior, we commend your servant, _____.
Acknowledge, we humbly beseech you, a sheep of your own fold, a lamb of your own flock, a sinner of your own redeeming.

Receive *him* into the arms of your mercy,
into the blessed rest of everlasting peace,
and into the glorious company of the saints in light.
Amen.

May his soul and the souls of all the departed,
through the mercy of God,
rest in peace.
Amen.

THE BOOK OF COMMON PRAYER 1979

•111 At a Vigil

(when the family and friends of the deceased come together for prayers prior to the funeral)

Dear Friends: It was our Lord Jesus himself who said "Come to me, all you who labor and are burdened, and I will give you rest." Let us pray, then, for our brother (sister) _____, that *he* may rest from *his* labors, and enter into the light of God's eternal sabbath rest.

Receive, O Lord, your servant, for *he* returns to you.
Into your hands, O Lord,
we commend our brother (sister) _____.

Wash *him* in the holy font of everlasting life, and clothe *him* in *his* heavenly wedding garment.
Into your hands, O Lord,
we commend our brother (sister) _____.

May *he* hear your words of invitation, "Come, you blessed of my Father."
Into your hands, O Lord,
we commend our brother (sister) _____.

May *he* gaze upon you, Lord, face to face, and taste the blessedness of perfect rest.
Into your hands, O Lord,
we commend our brother (sister) _____.

May angels surround *him*, and saints welcome *him* in peace.
Into your hands, O Lord,
we commend our brother (sister) _____.

(Silence)

Almighty God, our Father in heaven,
before whom live all who die in the Lord:
Receive our brother (sister) _____
into the courts of your heavenly dwelling place.
Let his *heart and soul now ring out in joy to you,*
O Lord, the living God, and the God of those who live.
This we ask through Christ our Lord.
Amen.

THE BOOK OF COMMON PRAYER 1979

•112 At a Funeral or Memorial Service

For our brother (sister) _____, let us pray to our Lord Jesus Christ who said, "I am the Resurrection and I am the Life."

(Silence)

Lord, you consoled Martha and Mary in their distress; draw near to us who mourn for _____, and dry the tears of those who weep.
Hear us, Lord.

You wept at the grave of Lazarus, your friend; comfort us in our sorrow.
Hear us, Lord.

You raised the dead to life; give to our brother (sister) eternal life.
Hear us, Lord.

You promised paradise to the thief who repented; bring our brother (sister) to the joys of heaven.

Hear us, Lord.

Our brother (sister) was washed in Baptism and anointed with the Holy Spirit; give *him* fellowship with all your saints.
Hear us, Lord.

He was nourished with your Body and Blood; grant *him* a place at the table in your heavenly kingdom.
Hear us, Lord.

Comfort us in our sorrows at the death of our brother (sister); let our faith be our consolation, and eternal life our hope.
Hear us, Lord.

(The Leader concludes with one of the following prayers:)

Lord Jesus Christ, we commend to you our brother (sister) _____, who was reborn by water and the Spirit in Holy Baptism. Grant that *his* death may recall to us your victory over death, and be an occasion for us to renew our trust in your Father's love. Give us, we pray, the faith to follow where you have led the way; and where you live and reign with the Father and the Holy Spirit, to the ages of ages. *Amen.*

(or)

Father of all, we pray to you for _____, and for all those whom we love but see no longer. Grant to them eternal rest. Let light perpetual shine upon them. May *his* soul and the souls of all the departed, through the mercy of God, rest in peace. *Amen.*

THE BOOK OF COMMON PRAYER 1979

•113 A Funeral Litany

Almighty God, you have knit your chosen people together in one communion, in the mystical body of your Son, Jesus Christ our Lord. Give to your whole Church in heaven and on earth your light and your peace.
Hear us, Lord.

Grant that all who have been baptized into Christ's death and resurrection may die to sin and rise to newness of life, and that through the grave and gate of death we may pass with him to our joyful resurrection.
Hear us, Lord.

Grant to us who are still on our pilgrimage, and who walk as yet by faith, that your Holy Spirit may lead us in holiness and righteousness all our days.
Hear us, Lord.

Grant to your faithful people pardon and peace, that we may be cleansed from all our sins and serve you with a quiet mind.

Hear us, Lord.

Grant to all who mourn a sure confidence in your loving care, that, casting all their sorrow on you, they may know the consolation of your love.
Hear us, Lord.

Give courage and faith to those who are bereaved, that they may have strength to meet the days ahead in the comfort of a holy and certain hope, and in the joyful expectation of eternal life with those they love.
Hear us, Lord.

Help us, we pray, in the midst of things we cannot understand, to believe and trust in the communion of saints, the forgiveness of sins, and the resurrection to life everlasting.
Hear us, Lord.

Grant us grace to entrust _____ to your never-failing love which sustained *him* in this life. Receive *him* into the arms of your mercy, and remember *him* according to the favor you bear for your people.
Hear us, Lord.

(The Leader concludes the litany with one of the following prayers:)

God, the generations rise and pass away before you. You are the strength of those who labor; you are the rest of the blessed dead. We rejoice in the company of your saints. We remember all who have lived in faith, all who have peacefully died, and especially those most dear to us who rest in you. Give us in your good time our portion with those who have trusted in you and have striven to do your holy will. To your name, with the Church on earth and the Church in heaven, we ascribe all honor and glory, now and forever. *Amen.*

God of all grace, you sent your Son, our Savior Jesus Christ, to bring life and immortality to light. We give you thanks because by his death Jesus destroyed the power of death and by his resurrection has opened the kingdom of heaven to all believers. Make us certain that because he lives we shall live also, and that neither death nor life, nor things present nor things to come shall be able to separate us from your love which is in Christ Jesus our Lord, who lives and reigns with you and the Holy Spirit, one God, now and forever. *Amen.*

THE LUTHERAN BOOK OF WORSHIP

War and Peace

•114 Christian Hope

The Christian hope is to live with confidence in newness and fullness of life, and to await the coming of Christ in glory, and the completion of God's purpose for the world.

This is our hope.

Earth's scattered isles and contured hills
which part the seas and mold the land,
and vistas newly seen from space
that show a world awesome and grand,
all wondrously write to sing:
take heart, take hope, the Lord is King!

We believe that Christ will come in glory to judge the living and the dead, raising us from death in the fullness of our being, that we may live with him in the communion of the saints.

This is our hope.

God's judgement passed on social ills
that thwart awhile his firm intent,
the flagging dreams of weary folk
whose brave new world lies torn and rent,
in painful form their message bring:
take heart, take hope, the Lord is King!

We believe in everlasting life, that new existence in which we are united with all the people of God, in the joy of fully knowing and loving God and each other.

This is our hope.

The constant care which Israel knew
alike in faith and faithlessness,
the subtle providence which guides
a pilgrim Church through change and stress,
inspire us gratefully to sing:
take heart, take hope, the Lord is King!

Our assurance as Christians is that nothing, not even death, shall separate us from the love of God which is in Christ Jesus our Lord.

This is our hope.

The light which shines through noble acts,
the quest for truth dispelling lies,
the grace of Christ renewed in us so love lives on and discord dies,
all blend their song, good news to bring:
take heart, take hope, the Lord is King!
Amen.

THE BOOK OF COMMON PRAYER 1979
HYMN STANZAS BY JEFFERY W. ROWTHORN*

•115 A Litany of Remembrance of All Peoples

Leader: Almighty God, we lift our hopes and prayers to you for all the peoples of the world; you know their condition and need as we do not, and our thoughts of them are poor because we have not cared enough to seek knowledge of them. Accept our prayers as we give expression to the concern in our hearts, and unite our wills with your own mighty intention of good for them.

Voice 1: We remember in silence before you
The peoples of Africa and the Middle East, ancient home of kings, birthplace of our culture, lands of bitter wrongs, of ignorance and fear, of disease and death; yet lands of promise, of great rivers and forests, mountains and plains, eager and strong men and women seeking and finding freedom, seeking and finding you.

(Silence)

Leader: Pour out your spirit upon people everywhere;

People: *And hasten the coming of your kingdom.*

Voice 2: We remember in silence before you
The peoples of Asia that their divisions may be healed, their
emancipation established, and their wisdom increased to
accept from other cultures only that which ennobles and
exalts.

(Silence)

Leader: Pour out your spirit upon people everywhere;

People: *And hasten the coming of your kingdom.*

Voice 3: We remember in silence before you
The peoples of Latin America, struggling upward from
ignorance and chaos into swift new achievement and
promise, yet hampered by tragic failures of government and
of enlightenment, that they may find their destiny anew in
your purpose.

(Silence)

Leader: Pour out your spirit upon people everywhere;

People: *And hasten the coming of your kingdom.*

Voice 4: We remember in silence before you
The peoples of Europe, many times crushed by war and
borne down with old divisions, that as ancient bearers of the
message of Christ they may again be inspired by your power
in all their common life.

(Silence)

Leader: Pour out your spirit upon people everywhere;

People: *And hasten the coming of your kingdom.*

Voice 5: We remember in silence before you
The peoples of the isles and continents of the seas, whose
new civilization has sprung up beside ancient tribal ways,
that in a day of swift travel and instant communication, they
may share what is deepest and best in the world's ways.

(Silence)

Leader: Pour out your spirit upon people everywhere;

People: *And hasten the coming of your kingdom.*

Voice 6: We remember in silence before you
Our own peoples on this continent, proud, tireless, groping
for new faith even as they seek to live up to the old; that
without condescension and overweening trust in their own
powers, they may humbly play their part in your holy pattern
for the world's life.

(Silence)

Leader: Pour out your spirit upon people everywhere;

People: *And hasten the coming of your kingdom.*

Leader: Grant, O God, that our imagination may be stretched to
enable us to share the poignant needs and vibrant exultation
of people everywhere; give us all to dwell in a large place,
and make your Church strong in every land, in every tongue,
for every people, in Christ Jesus our Lord.

All: *Amen.*

THE STUDENT PRAYER BOOK

•116 World Day of Prayer

God of Moses, saved in the river;
Save us today.

God of Israel, freed from Egypt, freed from the desert;
Save us today.

God of the slain Lamb, powerless Lion of Judah;
Save us today.

God of Nigeria and of Brazil, of the millions exploited by the black magic
of growth;
Save us today.

God of Cuba and of China, of the ambivalence of the revolution;
Save us today.

God of the Soviet Union and of the United States, dangerously powerful;
Save us today.

God of Sydney and of New York, of disappointment and new life;
Save us today.

God of the theologians, deceived by the wind of doctrine;

Save us today.

God of the bureaucrats, nervously searching for new programs;
Save us today.

God of Africa, of a growing church in a continent of exploitation;
Save us today.

God of Europe, of a shrinking church in a time of testing;
Save us today.

God of the religious people, caught in the projections of their own mind;
Save us today.

God of the conservatives, of the burning desire to save souls;
Save us today.

God of the liberals, dreaming of reform;
Save us today.

God of the radicals, dreaming of revolution;
Save us today.

God of the artists, dreaming and creating;
Save us today.

God of the technocrats, enslaved to the power they hold;
Save us today.

God of the exploiters, with their love of power;
Save us today.

God of the Christians, between faith and unfaith;
Save us today.

God of those who have never heard of Jesus Christ;
Save us today.

God of those who have heard of Christ but only see his people;
Save us today.

God of us – God of all,
surprise us anew with your faithfulness and save us today.
Save us today.
Amen.

WORLD COUNCIL OF CHURCHES*

•117 Global Responsibility

If the more than four billion people of the world could be represented in a community of just one hundred people:

Five of them would be United States citizens; the other ninety-five would be citizens of all the other countries.
In Christ there is no east or west,
In him no south or north,
But one great fellowship of love,
Throughout the whole wide earth.

The five Americans would own one-half of the money in the world; of the other ninety-five, seventy-five would own virtually nothing at all.
The first commandment is this: You shall love the Lord your God with all your heart, and with all your soul, and with all your mind, and with all your strength.

The five Americans would have fifteen times more material possessions than the other ninety-five put together.
And the second is this: You shall love your neighbor as yourself. There is no other commandment greater than these.

The five Americans would have seventy-two per cent more than the average daily food requirement; two-thirds of the remainder would be below minimum food standards, and many of them would be on a starvation diet.
Then he will say to those at his left hand, Depart from me, you cursed, into the eternal fire prepared for the devil and his angels; for I was hungry and you gave me no food, I was thirsty and you gave me no drink . . . Truly, I say to you, as you did not serve one of the least of these, you did not serve me. And they will go away into eternal punishment.

Cardinal Paul Silva of Santiago asks: "Do rich Christians know there are seven hundred million illiterates in the Third World, and two hundred million jobless, or that there are three hundred-ninety million near starvation and another one hundred-thirty million undernourished? . . . The rich fail even to suspect the frustrations, resentments, hate, and finally violence engendered by the contrast between those who have so much and the have-nots, between the ever-richer nations and the ever-poorer countries."
And Jesus said to the rich young man, There is still one thing you lack. Sell all you have and give the money to the poor. It will become treasure for you in heaven – and come, follow me.

(Silence)

Almighty God, awaken within us that still small voice we call the Christian conscience. Inform it with Scripture, confront it with human needs, quicken it with the compassion of Jesus; instill it with wisdom; and empower it with the Holy Spirit, that it may no longer merely make us feel guilty, but may cause us to spring forth from our beds of lethargy and become living hope and love to the world around us. Amen.

OFFICE OF CREATIVE MINISTRIES
MISSOURI AREA, UNITED METHODIST CHURCH

•118 A Litany of Resolve

(based on the preamble to the United Nations Charter)

It is our resolve to save succeeding generations from the scourge of war, which time and again in this century has brought untold sorrow to humankind.
   Lord, help us.

It is our resolve to reaffirm our faith in fundamental human rights, in the dignity and worth of the human person, in the equal rights of men and women and of nations large and small.
   Lord, help us.

It is our resolve to establish conditions under which justice and respect for the obligations arising from treaties and other sources of international law can be maintained, and to promote social progress and better standards of life in larger freedom.
   Lord, help us.

It is our resolve to unite our strength to maintain international peace and security, and to ensure that armed force shall not be used, save in the common interest.
   Lord, help us.

It is our resolve to employ international machinery for the promotion of the economic and social advancement of all peoples.
   Lord, help us.

And for these ends it is our resolve to practice tolerance and live together in peace with one another as good neighbors.
   Lord, help us. Amen.

THE ANGLICAN CATHEDRAL, LIVERPOOL
–PRAYERS FOR TODAY'S CHURCH

•119 A Litany of Human Rights

(based on the Universal Declaration of Human Rights adopted on December 10, 1948)

Almighty Lord, by whose holy urging the United Nations in our day, even while disputing with each other, are seeking a new world order of abiding law; grant to your Church everywhere insight to see this as your doing, and vigor to devote heart and mind to this great hope. So may the message of your love, which has freed men and women in every age, pervade and redeem even our halting efforts toward world peace, to the end that all the earth may discover and share the witness of your grace.

We thank you, Lord, for the gifts of wisdom and practicality by with leaders of the nations have set forth precepts to establish righteousness; as we dedicate these precepts anew to your glory, we dedicate ourselves also as instruments of your high purpose, to bring them to sound expression in the life of every people:
Everyone has the right to life, liberty, and the security of person.
Bless all your people, Lord, that they may know this holy freedom grounded in your gospel.

No one shall be held in slavery or servitude; slavery and the slave trade shall be prohibited in all their forms.
Bless all your people, Lord, that they may know this holy freedom grounded in your gospel.

No one shall be subjected to torture or to cruel, inhuman or degrading treatment or punishment.
Bless all your people, Lord, that they may know this holy freedom grounded in your gospel.

Everyone has the right to recognition everywhere as a person before the law.
Bless all your people, Lord, that they may know this holy freedom grounded in your gospel.

No one shall be subjected to arbitrary interference with privacy, family, home or correspondence, nor to attacks upon honor and reputation.
Bless all your people, Lord, that they may know this holy freedom grounded in your gospel.

Everyone has the right to a nationality.
Bless all your people, Lord, that they may know this holy freedom grounded in your gospel.

Everyone has the right to rest and leisure, including reasonable limitation of working hours and periodic holidays with pay.

Bless all your people, Lord, that they may know this holy freedom grounded in your gospel.

Everyone has the right to a standard of living adequate for the health and well-being of self and of family, including food, clothing, housing and medical care and necessary social services, and the right to security in the event of unemployment, sickness, disability, widowhood, old age or other lack of livelihood in circumstances beyond their control. Motherhood and childhood are entitled to special care and assistance; all children, whether born in or out of wedlock, shall enjoy the same social protection.
Bless all your people, Lord, that they may know this holy freedom grounded in your gospel.

Everyone has the right to education. Education shall be free, at least in the elementary and fundamental stages; elementary education shall be compulsory. Technical and professional education shall be made generally available, and higher education shall be equally accessible to all on the basis of merit.
Bless all your people, Lord, that they may know this holy freedom grounded in your gospel.

Education shall be directed to the full development of the human personality, and to the strengthening of respect for human rights and fundamental freedoms.
Bless all your people, Lord, that they may know this holy freedom grounded in your gospel.

Everyone has the right freely to practice their religion, to participate in the cultural life of the community, to enjoy the arts, and to share in scientific advancement and its benefits.
Bless all your people, Lord, that they may know this holy freedom grounded in your gospel.

Men and women of full age, without any limitations of race, nationality, or religion, have the right to marry and to found a family; the family is the natural and fundamental group unit of society, and is entitled to protection by society and the state.
Bless all your people, Lord, that they may know this holy freedom grounded in your gospel.

All people have duties to the community, in which alone the free and full development of their personalities is possible.
Bless all your people, Lord, that they may know this holy freedom grounded in your gospel.

O God, show us the solemn link between liberties and duties, that our responsibilities may equal our rights in society, and that great eagerness to serve may balance our expectation to be served. So may your kingdom come in freedom and in discipline, and your name be glorified in all justice and truth. *Amen.*

JOHN OLIVER NELSON
–THE STUDENT PRAYER BOOK

•120 World Peace

Remember, O Lord, the peoples of the world divided into many nations and tongues. Deliver us from every evil that gets in the way of your saving purpose; and fulfill the promise of peace to your people on earth, through Jesus Christ our Lord. *Amen.*

(Silence)

From the curse of war and the human sin that causes war;
O Lord, deliver us.

From pride that turns its back on you, and from unbelief that will not call you Lord;
O Lord, deliver us.

From national vanity that poses as patriotism; from loud-mouthed boasting and blind self-worship that admit no guilt;
O Lord, deliver us.

From the self-righteousness that will not compromise, and from selfishness that gains by the oppression of others;
O Lord, deliver us.

From the lust for money or power that drives people to kill;
O Lord, deliver us.

From trusting in the weapons of war, and mistrusting the councils of peace;
O Lord, deliver us.

From hearing, believing, and speaking lies about other nations;
O Lord, deliver us.

From groundless suspicions and fears that stand in the way of reconciliation;
O Lord, deliver us.

From words and deeds that encourage discord, prejudice, and hatred; from everything that prevents the human family from fulfilling your promise of peace;
O Lord, deliver us.

O God our Father: we pray for all your children on earth, of every nation and of every race; that they may be strong to do your will.
(Silence)

We pray for the church in the world.
Give peace in our time, O Lord.

For the United Nations;
Give peace in our time, O Lord.

For international federations of labor, industry, and commerce;
Give peace in our time, O Lord.

For departments of state, ambassadors, diplomats, and statesmen;
Give peace in our time, O Lord.

For worldwide agencies of compassion, which bind wounds and feed the hungry;
Give peace in our time, O Lord.

For all who in any way work to further the cause of peace and goodwill;
Give peace in our time, O Lord.

For common folk in every land who live in peace;
Give peace in our time, O Lord.

Eternal God: use us, even our ignorance and weakness, to bring about your holy will. Hurry the day when all people shall live together in your love; for yours is the kingdom, the power, and the glory forever. *Amen.*

THE WORSHIPBOOK

•121 Memorial Day

On this day our memories may be so painful that we cannot live with them. Yet we cannot, we dare not live without them. Let us pray that we may never forget, but always remember before God that in his sight war is evil and that to all who experience it, war is hell.

(Silence)

For leaders who send the young to war,
that their judgement be sound
and their motives be pure, we pray to the Lord.
Lord hear our prayer.

For soldiers who lay down their lives for others,
that the love which inspires their sacrifice

may be fulfilled in the love of Christ, we pray to the Lord.
Lord hear our prayer.

For soldiers who have been maimed or brutalized by war,
that our love for them may make their scars of no consequence
and make their brutality yield to the tenderness of returning love,
we pray to the Lord.
Lord hear our prayer.

For those who have been left behind,
that they may live on the strength of the love that they knew,
we pray to the Lord.
Lord hear our prayer.

For those who suffer most from war,
that the homeless, the orphaned, the hungry, and the innocent
may help us turn from warlike ways to accept God's gift of peace,
we pray to the Lord.
Lord hear our prayer.

(Silence)

Father, help us never to forget that war is evil and war is hell.
Help us to honor its dead and to pray for its victims who live on,
through him who for our sakes laid down his life,
even Jesus Christ our Lord.
Amen.

PRAYERS OF THE FAITHFUL

•122 At the Funeral of a Member of the Armed Forces

Let us ask our Father, who has seen his sons and daughters kill each other,
to take pity on us, to weep for us and to give _____ new life in Jesus, our
risen Lord.

(Silence)

For _____ whom we sent to war, and for all those we sent to die, that they
will live on in us, reminding us of the emptiness of hate, and of the peace
we cannot seem to attain, let us pray to the Lord.
Lord, hear our prayer.

For _____'s family and all the families shattered by war, that they will find in their community the healing strength of your love, let us pray to the Lord.
Lord, hear our prayer.

For _____'s friends and for everybody whose love has been killed in battle, that they will have the courage to continue giving the warmth of their hearts to those who are still alive, let us pray to the Lord.
Lord, hear our prayer.

For the veterans who have returned from World War I, World War II, Korea, Vietnam and Cambodia, and all the veterans of the world, that their memory of the act of war will be barren and their anger at the war's carnage will not stop until the world knows peace, let us pray to the Lord.
Lord, hear our prayer.

For those mutilated by war in their hearts and bodies, that they will find hope in him who created them whole, and support from us, our brother's keeper, let us pray to the Lord.
Lord, hear our prayer.

(Silence)

Father, grant to your servant _____, now with you, peace and everlasting life; help us bear our loss, and give us strength to pursue our quest for the unity and harmony of all your children, through Christ our Lord. Amen.

PRAYERS OF THE FAITHFUL

•123 Confession in a Nuclear Age

We confess our readiness to excuse and exempt ourselves from our nation's acts and policies.
Open us, Lord, to your truth and lead us to repentance.

We confess our nation's pride in winning the race to develop and use the first atomic bombs.
Open us, Lord, to your truth and lead us to repentance.

We confess our continuing national pride which has produced and perfected thousands of death-dealing nuclear weapons.
Open us, Lord, to your truth and lead us to repentance.

We confess our deep and abiding fear and hatred of our enemies which blinds this nation to your judgement of our own evil acts.
Open us, Lord, to your truth and lead us to repentance.

We confess that our nation clings to its stockpile of weapons to protect its power and wealth in the face of the earth's suffering millions.
Open us, Lord, to your truth and lead us to repentance.

We confess the national idolatry which allows our leaders to plan for the death of millions in a nuclear war in the name of national security and survival.
Open us, Lord, to your truth and lead us to repentance.
In Christ's name we pray.
Amen.

SOJOURNERS FELLOWSHIP*

•124 My People, I Am Your Security

My people, proclaim to the world not to trust in armaments for security.
My people, I am your security.
Lord, help us to be your people of peace.

Proclaim to the world not to fear the Great Powers, their stockpiled weapons and inflammatory rhetoric.
My people, I am your security.
Lord, help us to be your people of peace.

Proclaim to the world that missile silos and bomb factories are idols promising only destruction, not salvation.
My people, I am your security.
Lord, help us to be your people of peace.

Proclaim to the world that my kingdom is coming in power and not even the threat of nuclear war can destroy it.
My people, I am your security.
Lord, help us to be your people of peace.

Proclaim to the world that my kingdom will last for ever and all can share in its blessings even now.
My people, I am your security.
Lord, help us to be your people of peace.

Proclaim to the world to seek peace in the strength of the Prince of Peace.
My people, I am your security.
Lord, help us to be your people of peace.

Proclaim to the world that God is the Lord of time and will give you all time to repent and change your ways and live.
My people, I am your security.

Lord, help us to be your people of peace.

Proclaim to the world that all who are persecuted for their witness to peace share in God's own sufferings for the world.
My people, I am your security.
Lord, help us to be your people of peace.

Proclaim to the world that all who put their trust in God will find brothers and sisters to pray for them and work with them.
My people, I am your security.
Lord, help us to be your people of peace.

Proclaim to the world that all who work for peace will be blessed by God and called his sons and daughters.
My people, I am your security.
Lord, help us to be your people of peace.

Proclaim to the world that God's Spirit is given to all so that they may recognize God's image in each other and praise God's name together.
My people, I am your security.
Lord, help us to be your people of peace.

Proclaim to the world that now is the time for everyone to find their security in God's own community of love and peace.
My people, I am your security.
Lord, help us to be your people of peace.
Amen.

DAVID H. JANZEN*

•125 For This Fragile Earth, Our Island Home

Leader 1:   Lord, we cry out to you for a reversal in our nation's priorities. As we prepare for war, our disregard of the needs of the poor breeds violence in our cities. Bring us to repentance and change the hearts of our leaders.
Lord, in your mercy,

All: *Hear our prayer.*

Leader 2:   Lord, we cry out to you for all who suffer because conscience has led them to protest. We pray for an end to torture and other violations of human rights in the world.
Lord, in your mercy,

All: *Hear our prayer.*

Leader 1:   Lord, we cry out to you that all the nations, and especially the United States and the Soviet Union, will agree to stop testing and preparing to use nuclear weapons, as their contribution towards total disarmament and lasting peace.
Lord, in your mercy,

All: *Hear our prayer.*

Leader 2:   Lord, we cry out to you to hold back the 50,000 nuclear weapons that now exist from bringing about nuclear destruction.
Lord, in your mercy,

All: *Hear our prayer.*

Leader 1:   Lord, we cry out to you for all the victims of this nuclear age; recalling the horrors of Hiroshima and Nagasaki, we pray for those who suffer from the radiation effects, the trauma, or the memories of those two nightmare events.
Lord, in your mercy,

All: *Hear our prayer.*

Leader 2:   Lord, we cry out to you for those who earn their livelihood in military-related industries or professions. Show them how to break from their involvement with the ways of death.
Lord, in your mercy,

All: *Hear our prayer.*

Leader 1:   Lord, we cry out to you for the victims of nuclear testing around the world, especially in Nevada and Utah and in the South Pacific. Be with them as they struggle against the continued abuse of their homelands.
Lord, in your mercy,

All: *Hear our prayer.*

Leader 2: Lord, we cry out to you for the native peoples who have been forced to give up tribal lands for the testing and storage of nuclear weapons, especially the people of the Sioux in South Dakota and the aborigines of Australia.
Lord, in your mercy,

All: *Hear our prayer.*

Leader 1: Lord, we cry out to you for the many nations of the world who grow ever poorer under the domination of the superpowers and their all-consuming arms-race.
Lord, in your mercy,

All: *Hear our prayer.*

Leader 2: Lord, we cry out to you for those who are threatened by the poisoning of the environment, especially those who live near Three Mile Island in Harrisburg, Pennsylvania and the Love Canal in Buffalo, New York.
Lord, in your mercy,

All: *Hear our prayer.*

Leader 1: Lord, we cry out to you for ourselves that we may be better stewards and protectors of the earth's resources and more mindful of the environment which future generations will inherit.
Lord, in your mercy,

All: *Hear our prayer.*

Leader 2: Lord, we cry out to you for the whole human race, potential victims of a nuclear holocaust. In the midst of our fear, be present with us to grant us peace and sustain us in faith and hope and love.
Lord, in your mercy,

All: *Hear our prayer, through your Son our Savior Jesus Christ. Amen.*

SOJOURNERS FELLOWSHIP*

•126 For the Abolition of Nuclear Weapons

Leader 1: Let us accept our calling to be peacemakers in our day and in God's name covenant to work for the abolition of nuclear weapons.

(Silence)

Leader 1:   Let us covenant together to pray for peace:
To pray that God will hold back nuclear devastation so that we may turn from our folly and live;
To pray for our enemies and in this way bring them closer to us;
To pray that our faith in Christ's victory will triumph over the threat of nuclear war.

All: *Prince of Peace, help us all to pray for peace.*

Leader 2:   Let us covenant together to learn about peace:
To learn what the Bible teaches about peace so that we may study war no more;
To learn what makes for lasting peace between peoples and nations;
To learn what nuclear war would mean for our world and for our children.

All: *Prince of Peace, help us all to learn abou peace.*

Leader 1:   Let us covenant together to examine ourselves:
To discover how our lifestyle contributes to greed and hostility and ultimately to war;
To discover how our livelihoods depend increasingly on armaments and preparations for war;
To discover how our faith is compromised as we rely more and more on weapons of destruction.

All: *Prince of Peace, help us all to be honest about ourselves for the sake of peace.*

Leader 2:   Let us covenant together to spread the gospel of peace:
To tell our families and friends about the dangers of nuclear weapons;
To tell our churches about the claims of Christ upon our actions and our lives;
To tell our communities that there can be no protection against a nuclear attack.

All: *Prince of Peace, help us all to be witnesses for peace.*

Leader 1:   Let us covenant together to work for peace:
To work to persuade our leaders that nuclear war is an unthinkable act;
To work to persuade the Church that nuclear war is a sinful deed;
To work to persuade the world that nuclear war is a terminal disease.

200

All: *Prince of Peace, help us all to be peacemakers in our day.*

(Silence)

All: *In God's name we solemnly covenant to work for the abolition of nuclear weapons and the threat of nuclear war, and with God's help to seek peace and to pursue it in every aspect of our lives.*
We make this covenant, trusting in the strength of the Prince of Peace, even Jesus Christ our Lord. Amen.

SOJOURNERS MAGAZINE*

•127 God of the Coming Age

Leader: God of the coming age,

Men: *With eager longing*
     all creation waits for transformation:

Women: *In ardent hope*
      we yearn for our redemption.

Leader: Powerful Presence of God, we ask for hope, for ability
      to believe beyond the evidence,
      to wait with patience when the cause seems lost,
      to hold with steady confidence the dream
        of a world made healthy and whole.

      God of the coming age,

Men: *With eager longing*
     all creation waits for transformation:

Women: *In ardent hope*
      we yearn for our redemption.

Leader: Merciful Presence of God, we ask forgiveness.
      Too much we have given our allegiance
        to governments and corporations.
      Too often we have trusted commentators
        and journalists.

      God of the coming age,

Men: *With eager longing*
     all creation waits for transformation:

| Women: | In ardent hope |
| | *we yearn for our redemption.* |

Leader:	Too completely we have served the interests
	of earth's old administration,
	corrupt and soon to fall from power.
	Too little have we given ourselves to the
	causes that promise a world of equity and peace.

God of the coming age,

| Men: | *With eager longing* |
| | *all creation waits for transformation:* |

| Women: | *In ardent hope* |
| | *we yearn for our redemption.* |

Leader:	Life-giving Presence of God, we ask for signs
	of the age to come:
	a new generation of leaders in the struggle for peace;
	a way of balancing the earth's food and its peoples'
	longing for daily bread

God of the coming age,

| Men: | *With eager longing* |
| | *all creation waits for transformation:* |

| Women: | *In ardent hope* |
| | *we yearn for our redemption.* |

Leader:	A cleansing of humanity's patterns
	so that rivers are clean again
	and the air made fit to breathe again;
	the breaking of the power of sickness
	and calamity, of oppression and cruelty,
	so that all may come to fullness of life.

God of the coming age,

| Men: | *With eager longing* |
| | *all creation waits for transformation:* |

| Women: | *In ardent hope* |
| | *we yearn for our redemption.* |

| All: | Amen. |

KEITH WATKINS
BASED ON ROMANS 8:18-25*

202

Notes

Wherever an asterisk (*) appears at the end of any of the litanies in this book, it signifies that additional information can be found in what follows. The number to the left of the page denotes the particular litany which is being commented on here. All the tunes mentioned in these Notes can be found in the Lutheran Book of Worship *unless otherwise·indicated.*

6. This litany is based on "The Hartford Appeal" which was issued by an ecumenical gathering of theologians and church leaders who met at the Hartford Seminary in Connecticut in January 1975. In their appeal they rejected the thirteen contemporary "heresies" or "themes" mentioned in the course of the litany. A special symposium on "The Hartford Appeal" was published in the journal *Worldview* in the summer of 1975. The concluding collect in the litany is taken from the *Book of Common Prayer 1979*.

8. *Models for Ministers I,* issue of October 6, 1974.

15. This cycle of intercessions would be especially effective if used on seven consecutive days; it could, however, be used on the same day of the week over a period of seven weeks. It is the work of the *Joint Liturgical Group*, a British ecumenical body which brings together representatives of the Anglican, Roman Catholic, Methodist, Baptist, and United Reformed (Congregationalist – Presbyterian) Churches, the Church of Scotland, and the Churches of Christ.

19. This may be sung to the tune *Deidre* which is found in the (Episcopal) *Hymnal 1940* at no. 268 (stanza 6 only).

20. This comes from *Personal Prayers* (1733), the first collection of prayers to be published by John Wesley.

26. The words read by the person leading this litany are the closing lines of W. H. Auden's *For the Time Being: A Christmas Oratorio* (1945). They have been set to music by Ronald Arnatt; the tune *St. Louis New* may be found in *More Hymns and*

Spiritual Songs (© 1971, 1977, Walton Music Corporation). The hymn stanzas in this litany may be sung to *Chesterfield (Richmond)*.

33. These words are set to the tune *Lytlington* in the (Episcopal) *Hymnal 1940* at no. 466.

38. This hymn was written by Dr. Fosdick to mark the dedication of Riverside Church in New York City; it was first sung at the opening service on October 5, 1930. It is widely sung to the tune *Cwm Rhondda*.

39. *Models for Ministers I,* issue of August 24, 1975.

44. *Models for Ministers I,* issue of January 25, 1976. The second half of the litany consists largely of the familiar prayer of St. Francis of Assisi which begins, "Lord, make me an instrument of your peace."

51. *Liturgy,* issue of March 1973 (Vol. 18, No. 3). This is the journal of the Liturgical Conference, an ecumenical association dedicated to the renewal of the Church's life and worship. *Liturgy* now appears four times a year.

54. This litany was first used at the Anglican Cathedral in Liverpool, England. The final blessing is taken from the *Book of Occasional Services* where it is used at the conclusion of a service to celebrate the anniversary of a marriage.

56. Psalm 112 is an "alphabetical psalm"; in the Hebrew original each successive line begins with a different letter of the alphabet. This unusual characteristic is reproduced here in the English version which is taken from *Family Worship in the Parish* by Donald Orin Wiseman.

69. Richard Granville Jones' hymn, written in 1964, was first used at a meeting of the Methodist Synod in Sheffield, England; it may be sung to the tune *Dix*.

71. This prayer by Reinhold Niebuhr, here slightly adapted, was first published in the worship material in *Hymns for Worship,* prepared for the Student Christian Movement, edited by Ursula M. Niebuhr, and published by Association Press in 1939.

79. The hymn stanzas may be sung to *Monkland* which is in the (Episcopal) *Hymnal 1940* or to Daniel Moe's contemporary tune *Williams Bay*.

85-86. *Models for Ministers I,* issues of June 29, 1975 (Litany 85) and July 4, 1976 (Litany 86).

87. *Liturgy,* issue of May 1970 (Vol. 15, No. 5).

90. Queen Elizabeth II ascended the throne on February 6, 1952 and her Silver Jubilee was officially celebrated on June 7, 1977. This litany in its original form was used in the Service of Thanksgiving held that day in St. Paul's Cathedral, London.

94. In the *Lutheran Book of Worship* the hymn used in this litany is set to the early American folk tune *Kedron*. Any other appropriate tune in Long Meter may also be used.

96. The opening measures of *Veni Emmanuel* may be used if the response after each period of silence is sung.

98. The words recited by the congregation in the course of this litany make up the *General Confession which has formed part of the Anglican liturgy since the second Book of Common Prayer* (1552).

101. This is a conflation of two litanies included in *Prayers from the Burned-Out City*. Both the *Litany for the City* and the *Litany for the Poor* are clearly inspired in their radical content by Jesus' parable of the sheep and the goats (Matthew 25:31-46). There the great judgment is dependent on one thing and one thing only: "Truly, I say to you, as you did it (not) to one of the least of these my brethren, you did it (not) to me."

108. This litany was used at a service held at the Anglican Cathedral in Liverpool, England; the concluding collect is taken from the *Book of Common Prayer 1979*.

114. The hymn stanzas may be sung to the tune *Melita*.

116. This litany was prepared for the Bangkok Conference which was held in Thailand in 1972. It was later published in the September 21, 1975 issue of *Models for Ministers I*.

123-126 These litanies are all based on material first used by the Sojourners Fellowship of Washington, D.C., a community dedicated to peace and reconciliation. Litany 124 is taken from a prophecy given by the Lord to David H. Janzen after he had fasted and prayed in the summer of 1978 about a Christian witness against the arms race. This prophecy was published in *Sojourners* (Vol. 8, No. 1, January 1979: p. 19). The title of Litany 125 is taken from Eucharistic Prayer C in the *Book of Common Prayer 1979*. Litany 126 is based on the *New Abolitionist Covenant*, the text of which appeared in the August 1981 issue of *Sojourners* (Vol. 10, No. 8, pp. 18-19). *Sojourners* is now published monthly (with the exception of July and August).

127. This litany was used by the author when he preached at Yale Divinity School in the spring of 1983. Professor Watkins teaches worship at Christian Theological Seminary in Indianapolis, Indiana.

Bibliography

The litanies in this collection were compiled from the following sources which are listed alphabetically in the form in which they appear at the end of each particular litany:

Acts of Devotion, compiled by F. W. Dwelly. S.P.C.K., London, 1928.

Lancelot Andrewes, Bishop of Winchester: *Preces Privatae;* selections from the translation by F.E. Brightman, M.A., edited, with an introduction, by A.E. Burn, D.D., Methuen and Co., London, 1908.

The Alternative Service Book 1980: Services authorized for use in the Church of England in conjunction with *The Book of Common Prayer* (1662). Cambridge University Press, William Clowes (Publishers) Ltd., and S.P.C.K., 1980.

W.H. Auden: *For the Time Being – A Christmas Oratorio.* Random House, New York, 1945.

The Authorized Daily Prayer Book, Revised Edition, prepared by Joseph H. Hertz, late Chief Rabbi of the British Empire. Bloch Publishing Co., New York, 1948 (5709).

John Baillie: *A Diary of Private Prayer.* Charles Scribner's Sons, New York, 1949.

William Barclay: *Epilogues and Prayers.* Abingdon Press, New York and Nashville, 1963.

William Barclay: *Prayers for Help and Healing.* Harper and Row, New York and Evanston, 1968.

William Barclay: *Prayers for the Christian Year.* Harper and Row, New York and Evanston, 1965.

The Rev. Martha Blacklock (Mother Thunder Mission), St. Clement's Episcopal Church, 423 West 46th Street, New York, NY 10036.

The Book of Catholic Worship (1966). The Liturgical Conference, 2900 Newton Street N.W., Washington, D.C. 20018.

The Book of Common Prayer (1928). The Church Pension Fund, New York.

The Book of Common Prayer (1979). The Church Hymnal Corporation and Seabury Press, New York.

A Book of Family Prayers, prepared by Gabe Huck. Seabury Press, New York, 1979.

The Book of Occasional Services. The Church Hymnal Corporation, New York, 1979.

Walter Russell Bowie: *Lift Up Your Hearts,* Enlarged Edition. Abingdon Press, New York and Nashville, 1956.

Bread for the World, 32 Union Square East, New York, NY 10003.

Carl F. Burke: *Treat Me Cool, Lord.* Association Press, New York, 1968.

Robert W. Castle, Jr.: *Prayers from the Burned-Out City.* Sheed and Ward, New York, 1968.

Church of South India: *The Book of Common Worship.* Oxford University Press, London, 1963.

Contemporary Prayers for Public Worship, edited by Caryl Micklem. S.C.M. Press, Ltd., London, 1967.

The Covenant of Peace – A Liberation Prayer Book, compiled by John P. Brown and Richard L. York. Morehouse-Barlow Co., New York (now Wilton, Connecticut), 1971.

The Cuddesdon College Office Book, Revised Edition. Oxford University Press, London, 1961.

The Daily Office Revised (with other prayers and services), edited by Ronald C.D. Jasper on behalf of the Joint Liturgical Group. S.P.C.K., London, 1978.

Lucien Deiss: *Come, Lord Jesus* (French original: *Prières Bibliques).* World Library Publications, Inc., 5040 North Ravenswood, Chicago, IL 60640.

Devotional Services for Public Worship, compiled by John Hunter. J.M. Dent, Ltd., London, 1903.

Early Christian Prayers (French original: *Prières des Premiers Chrétiens),* edited by A. Hamman, O.F.M., translated by Walter Mitchell. Longmans, Green and Co., Ltd., London, 1961.

Ember Prayers: A Collection of Prayers for the Ministry of the Church, compiled by John Neale. S.P.C.K., London, 1965.

Harry Emerson Fosdick: *A Book of Public Prayers.* Harper and Bros., New York, 1959.

Further Anglican Liturgies (1968-1975), edited by Colin Buchanan. Grove Books, Bramcote, Nottingham, 1975.

Gates of Prayer: The New Union Prayer Book (Weekdays, Sabbaths and Festivals: Services and Prayers for Synagogue and Home). Central Conference of American Rabbis, New York, 1975 (5735).

Norman C. Habel: *Interrobang – A Bunch of Unanswered Prayers and Unlimited Shouts.* Fortress Press, Philadelphia, 1969.

Larry Hard: *Contemporary Altar Prayers (Volume 3).* C.S.S. Publishing Co., Inc., Lima, Ohio, 1973.

David Head: *He Sent Leanness – A Book of Prayers for the Natural Man.* The Macmillan Co., New York, 1959.

Raymond Hockley: *Intercessions at Holy Communion on Themes for the Church's Year.* A.R. Mowbray and Co., Ltd., London and Oxford, 1980.

The Hymnal of the Protestant Episcopal Church in the United States of America – 1940. The Church Hymnal Corporation, New York, 1943.

Irish Litanies: text and translation, edited from the manuscripts by the Rev. Charles Plummer, M.A. Henry Bradshaw Society, Volume 62 (1924), printed by Harrison and Sons, Ltd., London, 1925.

The Kingdom, the Power and the Glory: Services of Praise and Prayer for Occasional Use in Churches (American Edition of *The Grey Book).* Oxford University Press, New York, 1933.

Kyrie Eleison: Two Hundred Litanies, compiled by Benjamin F. Musser. The Newman Bookshop, Westminster, Maryland, 1945.

Laudamus: Services and Songs of Praise, edited by Jeffery Rowthorn, Bruce Neswick and W. Thomas Jones. Yale Divinity School, 409 Prospect Street, New Haven, Connecticut 06510.

Liturgy, now published quarterly by The Liturgical Conference, 2900 Newton Street N.W., Washington, D.C. 20018.

The Liturgy in English, edited by Bernard Wigan. Oxford University Press, London, 1962.

The Lutheran Book of Worship. Augsburg Publishing House, Minneapolis, 1978.

The Methodist Service Book. The Methodist Publishing House, Wimbeldon, London, 1936.

H. Miller: *Prayers for Daily Use.* Harper and Bros., New York, NY, 1957.

Models for Ministers I. World Library Publications, Inc., 5040 North Ravenswood, Chicago, Illinois 60640.

Modern Anglican Liturgies (1958-1968), edited by Colin Buchanan. Oxford University Press, London, 1968.

Modern Liturgy, now published eight times a year by Resource Publications, 7291 Coronado Drive, San Jose, California 95129.

Monday's Ministries: The Ministry of the Laity, edited by Raymond Tiemeyer. Parish Life Press, Philadelphia, 1979.

The Office of Creative Ministries, Missouri Area, United Methodist Church, P.O. Box 733, Columbia, Missouri 65205.

Huub Oosterhuis: *Your Word is Near – Contemporary Christian Prayers,* translated by N. D. Smith. Newman Press, New York, 1968 (Dutch original: 1961).

Praise God: Common Prayer at Taizé (French original: *La Louange des Jours,* 1971), translated by Emily Chisholm. Oxford University Press, New York, 1977.

Praise Him! A Prayerbook for Today's Christian, edited by William G. Storey. Ave Maria Press, Notre Dame, Indiana, 1973.

Pray Like This: Materials for the Practice of Dynamic Group Prayer, compiled by William G. Storey. Fides Publishers, Inc., Notre Dame, Indiana, 1973.

Prayers and Other Resources for Public Worship, compiled by Horton Davies and Morris Slifer. Abingdon Press, Nashville, 1976.

Prayers for a New World, compiled and edited by John W. Suter. Charles Scribner's Sons, New York, 1964.

Prayers for Today's Church, edited by Dick Williams. Augsburg Publishing House, Minneapolis, 1977.

Prayers for Use at the Alternative Services, compiled and adapted by David Silk. A.R. Mowbray and Co. Ltd., London and Oxford, 1980.

Prayers in Community (Volume 1 of *Contemporary Prayer),* edited by Thierry Maertens and Marguerite De Bilde, translated by Jerome J. DuCharme. Fides Publishers, Inc., Notre Dame, Indiana, 1974.

Prayers of the Faithful (for Sundays and Solemnities of Cycles A, B and C). Pueblo Publishing Co., New York, 1977.

Prayers, Thanksgivings, Litanies: prepared by the Standing Liturgical Commission of the Episcopal Church *(Prayer Book Studies 25).* Church Hymnal Corporation, New York, 1973.

The Psalms: A New Translation, translated from the Hebrew and arranged for singing to the psalmody of Joseph Gelineau. Paulist Press, New York, 1965.

The Roman Missal, revised by decree of the Second Vatican Council and published by authority of Pope Paul VI; English translation prepared by the International Commission on English in the Liturgy. Catholic Book Publishing Co., New York, 1974.

Rural People at Worship, compiled by Edward K. Ziegler. Agricultural Missions, Inc., New York, 1943.

Scripture Services: 18 Bible Themes, edited for group use by John Gallen, S.J. The Liturgical Press, Collegeville, Minnesota, 1963.

Kay Smallzried: *Litanies for Living – Spilled Milk*. Oxford University Press, New York, 1964.

Sojourners, 1309 L Street N.W., Washington, D.C. 20005.

Michael Sopocko: *God is Mercy,* translated from the Polish by the Marian Fathers. Grail Publications, St. Meinrad, Indiana, 1955.

The Student Prayer Book, edited and written by a Haddam House committee under the chairmanship of John Oliver Nelson. Association Press, New York, 1953.

Table Prayers, compiled by Mildred Tengbom. Augsburg Publishing House, Minneapolis, 1977.

The Taizé Office (French original: *Office de Taizé,* 1963), translated by Anthony Brown. Faith Press, London, 1966.

Carl T. Uehling: *Prayers for Public Worship.* Fortress Press, Philadelphia, 1972.

John Wesley's Prayers, edited by Frederick C. Gill. Epworth Press, London, 1951.

Herbert B. West: *Stay with me, Lord – A Man's Prayers.* Seabury Press, New York, 1974.

With One Voice – Prayers from around the World, compiled by Robert M. Bartlett. Thomas Y. Crowell Co., New York, 1961.

Elmer N. Witt: *Help It All Make Sense, Lord.* Concordia Publishing House, St. Louis and London, 1972.

Elmer N. Witt: *Time to Pray: Daily Prayers for Youth.* Concordia Publishing House, St. Louis, undated (preface dated St. Luke's Day, 1959).

Worldview, published by the Council on Religion and International Affairs, 170 East 64th Street, New York, NY 10021.

The Worshipbook. Westminster Press, Philadelphia, 1970.

Worship for Today – Suggestions and Ideas, edited by Richard Jones. Epworth Press, London, 1968.

Worship Services for Special Occasions, compiled and edited by Norman L. Hersey. World Publishing Co., New York and Cleveland, 1970.